They said we were isolated

Joanna Talberg

# They said we were isolated
My life at Top Farm on Tasmania's west coast

This book is dedicated to my parents, Mum and Yang,
Barbara Wellesley Talberg née Chapman,
Group Captain Wilbur Herbert Talberg OBE

*They said we were isolated: My life at Top Farm on Tasmania's west coast*
ISBN 978 1 76109 541 2
Copyright © text Joanna Talberg 2023

First published 2023 by
**Ginninderra Press**
PO Box 3461 Port Adelaide 5015
www.ginninderrapress.com.au

# Contents

| | |
|---|---|
| 1: At the end of the track | 7 |
| 2: His tail was on fire | 16 |
| 3: Putting down roots | 30 |
| 4: An amateur archaeologist | 40 |
| 5: Only a leech | 52 |
| 6: Lost in white water | 63 |
| 7: 'We must call him Whisky' | 72 |
| 8: A fish on the end of a line | 86 |
| 9: No mail | 99 |
| 10: Paddling upstream | 109 |
| 11: The army comes to Top Farm | 120 |
| 12: Bareback no hands | 131 |
| 13: A thylacine in the forest? | 147 |
| 14: From landed gentry to garbage man | 152 |
| 15: Three tiny rosebuds | 159 |
| Notes | 163 |

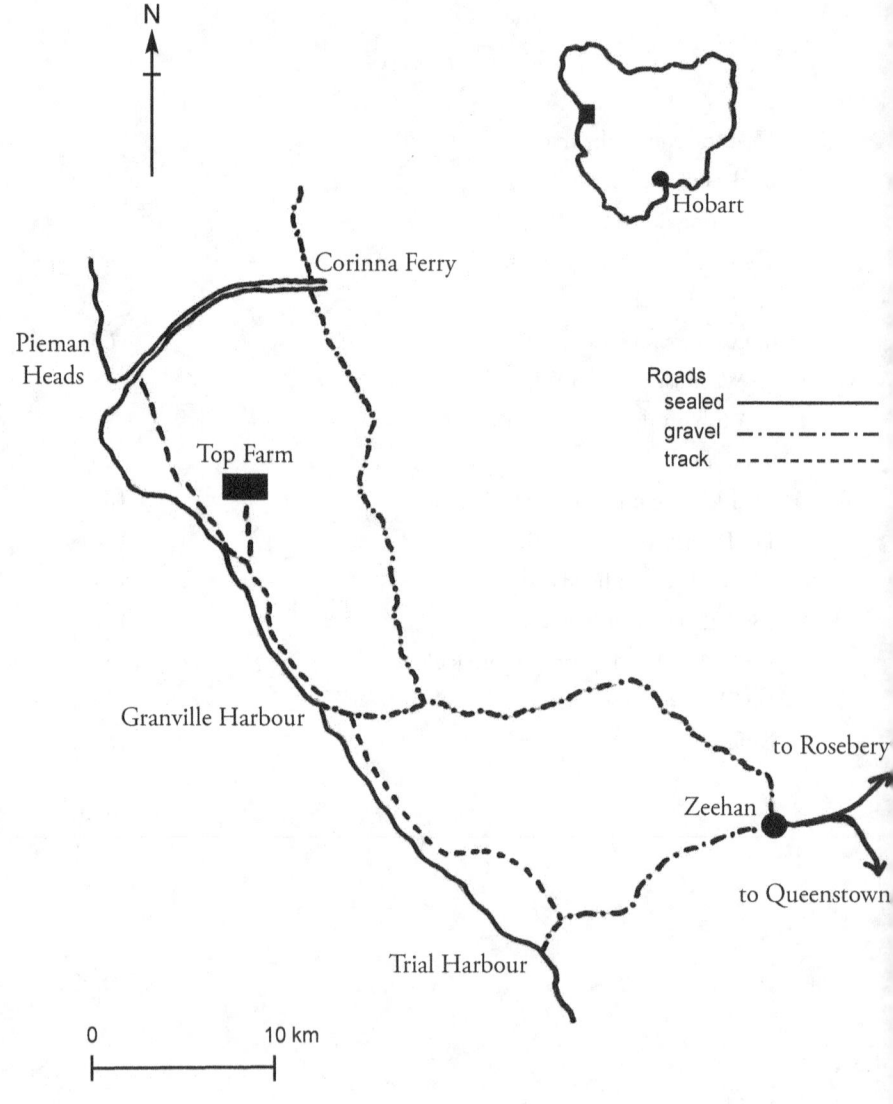

*Top Farm area, 1970s.*

# 1

# At the end of the track

Tingling with excitement, I slam the passenger door of the Land Rover behind me and grin at Peter in the driver's seat. It's 1974 and we're in Zeehan, a mining town on the west coast of Tasmania. My husband's tanned face is lit up with boyish excitement. He's eager to take me out to our new home, a neglected cattle property called Top Farm that's situated on the coast, north-west of the town. He's already spent three weeks on the place with our partner, Bob Werner, while I've been staying with my parents in Canberra.

It's a chilly, bleak afternoon, and gusts of wind and rain pummel the vehicle as we drive out of Zeehan. The bitumen ends at the town's outskirts, where a ramshackle weatherboard cottage leans so far sideways it threatens to fall into the vacant block next door. I cling to the metal dashboard as the vehicle creaks and rattles up a hill on which low shrubs and a few spindly trees grow. Further on, in a gravelled clearing in the scrub, there's an old mineshaft topped by a windlass. A caravan is parked nearby, an old-fashioned caravan with a rounded roof and peeling paint. The words 'miners wanted' are scrawled on a crooked sign stuck in the ground.

This lean country is not what I'd expected. I frown and tighten my fingers on the dashboard as Peter zigzags around potholes in the track.

A friend in Canberra had asked, 'Jo, why are you going to the west coast of Tasmania? It's the end of the world.'

I'd waved my hands in the air and said, 'I always knew when I married Peter we'd end up in the country.'

The question hovers in my mind as we pass more abandoned mine workings, stands of straggling trees and a cemetery set among the scrub. Empty black and white beer cans litter the edges of the track as we travel across open plains covered with dense clumps of a coarse plant.

'What's that plant?'

'Buttongrass,' Peter tells me. 'It's a sedge. Grows all over the west coast, usually on poorly drained soil.'

\*

I'd grown up as a sheltered only child and had leaped out of the nest at twenty and flown off to Papua New Guinea, South America and Europe seeking adventure. Now, heading through forlorn country towards a remote property where we planned to settle, my heart judders. Top Farm offers a different kind of adventure – tough, gritty adventure for the rest of my life.

Peter's home was a cocoa plantation in PNG. Isolated rural life is as familiar to him as ballet lessons had been to me as a child. A practical man who can turn his hand to any outdoor, agricultural task from fixing a tractor to building a shed, Peter is a bit of a loner, yet talkative and funny when with friends. He has olive skin, jet-black hair and a wicked sense of humour, which is to ease many situations in the future – except on the occasions when I want to throttle him.

\*

The groan and grind of the engine fills my ears and Peter's left hand constantly changes gears beside me. Occasional gusts of wind zoom in through the air vent below the windscreen, dropping cold drizzle onto my jeans. I shiver and pull the vent closed with a muffled screech. I sit back in my seat, trying to feel sanguine. It's cosy in the cabin of the vehicle with the wind and drizzle outside, and I like the old Land Rover. It's battered around the edges but as strong and solid as a draught horse.

I glance at Peter, at his tanned face, straight nose and determined, jutting chin. Black-rimmed glasses frame his blue eyes. I'm thrilled we're together again. I'd missed him so much in Canberra.

'I missed you,' he says, glancing at me.

I blink. It's happening again, thinking each other's thoughts. My heart swells. I lean over and kiss his cheek. 'I missed you, too.'

Around a corner we see a vehicle coming towards us along the stony track, the first car we've encountered on this lonely road. Bright red and shiny, the car is a spot of colour in this grey landscape. Peter waves as the vehicle passes us, and the driver waves back.

'Who was that?'

'Dunno. Everyone waves on the west coast.'

Further on, he gestures to the surrounding country and touches my arm. 'Well?' he asks. 'What do you think?' His eyebrows are frowning above his glasses, and I see the worry in his eyes.

I say nothing but try to smile, realising my husband is as apprehensive as I am, although for a different reason. He's already grown to love Top Farm – and is afraid I won't.

\*

The salty smell of the ocean fills my nostrils as we bump and bounce along a winding, coastal track. It's dotted with boulders buried in the gravel that tip the Land Rover from one side to the other. The pitch of the engine changes all the time. Bracken fern and heath-like plants line the track, and I recognise banksia and wattle trees growing among the hardy, wind-pruned vegetation. Masses of yellow flowers cover many of the shrubs. There are pyramid-shaped rocks everywhere, and between them, I catch glimpses of distant sand dunes glowing in the sun.

I sit up, newly alert. This country is wild but no longer bleak. Gulls wheel and cry overhead and, when we turn a corner, a sprinkling of pink and yellow wildflowers greets us.

'Look,' Peter says, pointing to a bird wading in a pond near the road. 'It's a white-faced heron but people around here call them blue cranes.'

We turn a corner and enter a different world, a rural idyll of fat cattle grazing on green pastures, out of place in this rugged land. I blink in surprise at the change in the scenery. The drizzle has ceased and the sun peeps through the clouds. Even the fragrance of the air is different. Softer, more gentle.

'The Bottom Farm,' Peter says. 'Granville Estates is its proper name. Our place and the Bottom Farm are the only grazing properties in the district.'

The cattle lift their heads and gaze at us, swishing their tails. Peter tells me that the wives of owners Don Smith and Jim Reynolds live in town with their children. That isn't for me. I'm eager to grasp everything this new life has to offer, 'the full catastrophe', to misquote that exuberant character Zorba the Greek in the 1964 film of the same name.

We leave the gentle pastures behind and a new feeling of exhilaration surges through my body as I look out at the landscape of rocks and tough plants. I like this coastal country. I slide open the passenger window. Boulders and stones shoulder aside sparse grasses and hardy shrubs fighting for a living between them. Lichens that look eons old spot many of the rocks, but I'm surprised to see the fragile new leaves of a tiny plant shooting up in a crevice between two boulders.

The track leads us down a slope into Granville Harbour. *Harbour?* It's an inlet in a rugged coastline, that's all. Waves crash onto rocks and sea spray shoots high into the air. Pieces of driftwood and massive piles of giant brown spaghetti, called bull kelp, are strewn over the rocky edges of the inlet. Fishing shacks built of corrugated iron and scrap timber line both sides of the track. There's no store or jetty.

'The shacks are owned by west coasters who come for weekends,' Peter says, in answer to my question.

'Where from?'

'Zeehan, Queenstown or even the north coast. I was talking to a bloke from Devonport last weekend. He was down for a few days to catch some crayfish and see his mates.'

The large, green leaves of pumpkin vines surround one of the shacks like water around an island. We pull up outside.

'This is Schultzie's,' my husband says. 'He makes wine with his pumpkins.'

Shouts of laughter reach our ears as we climb out of the vehicle and swish through the sea of pumpkin leaves to the front door, which is open.

'G'day, Schultzie,' says Peter, peering in.

'Pete. Come in. You must be Joanna,' says our host, who, I learn, is a miner from Rosebery.

Three other men stop talking and jump up from their chairs as soon as they realise a girl has joined them. Peter introduces me to Colin Casey, his brother Johnny and Viv Coleman.

'Sit here, Joanna,' says Johnny, pulling up a spare chair.

'No, here,' puts in Viv, offering his own chair to me.

'Hello. Thanks.' I don't know which chair to choose, and hesitate nervously, grateful to both men. Eventually I sit down on the spare chair. I clasp my hands together on my lap and take in my surroundings as the men resume their conversation about the best time of year for abalone.

Schultzie opens a can of beer and offers it to me. 'Sorry, Joanna. Beer's all I've got.' It isn't the season for pumpkin wine, apparently.

There's a fireplace at one end of the room, a table in the middle and a neat set of cooking implements hanging from hooks on the wall: a potato masher, a colander and several pairs of fire-blackened tongs. The shack is clean and cosy, and the fragrant smell of woodsmoke hangs in the air, a smell which takes me back to bush picnics with my parents and cooking chops over a fire. I sip my beer happily and settle into my seat.

Colin and Johnny Casey are as unalike as brothers can be. Colin is a tall, tanned, handsome man, while Johnny is stockier and has a swarthy complexion and an easy manner. Viv is a big bloke with a gentle face, a retired miner from Williamsford with thin grey hair who's wearing a darned brown jumper.

Johnny is sitting beside me. 'You've been staying in Canberra?'

'Yes. With my parents.' I pause. 'They live there,' I add, mentally kicking myself for stating the obvious. I don't know what else to say. Nor, I guess, does he. Johnny and the others are hardy, west coast bushmen and fishermen and I understand their reticence about trying to talk to a new chum from faraway Canberra.

The easy talk flows around me, moving from Tasmanian devils and whether they're becoming bolder to the giant crayfish caught by a fisherman the day before. My heart beats faster and I lean forward in my chair as interest in this new world stirs deep inside me. Every one of my senses is heightened. I've fallen down the rabbit hole into a place as different from Canberra as crayfish are from croissants, and I want to know more.

Colin tells the story of a bloke whose vehicle was swamped on Four Mile Beach. 'Don't get bogged on the beach, mate,' he says to Peter. 'If you do, the incoming tide'll roll your vehicle over like a Dinky toy and fill it with sand.'

Peter nods knowingly, but I don't. My eyebrows shoot up. 'Really?'

'Happened last week,' puts in Johnny. 'The waves turned the vehicle over and over.'

'And it's still there, lying on the beach,' Viv says.

Little do we know the drama this beach has in store for us in a few months' time.

*

By the time we drive away from Schultzie's, dusk has turned to darkness. The boom of the surf is loud inside the vehicle. The headlights light up the rocky track ahead. Peter swings the wheel over to take a sharp turn and we crawl up a slope – but at the top, the front wheels plop over a bank and we lurch forward. I grab the dashboard as the headlights shine into empty space. My handbag shoots onto the floor, spilling its contents. Peter swears and stands on the brakes. The vehicle bellies, rocks back and forth, and stills.

'Bloody idiot,' he says, furious with himself. 'Now we'll have to walk back to Granville. Hop out Joanna, slowly, without rocking the vehicle. I'll pick up your things.'

He fishes for a torch on the shelf in front of my seat. I watch through the open door as he picks up my lipstick, comb, purse, a notebook and pen and a lucky tiki charm he'd bought for me in South America. He slips them into my bag and passes it out to me.

As we walk back to Granville, the beam of the torch falls on rocky, gravel-strewn ground.

'It's rough.' He takes my arm. 'Be careful.' His voice is low and subdued. Contrite.

Half an hour later, Johnny Casey hauls the Land Rover backwards off the bank with his own vehicle and, with a cheeky grin, slaps Peter on the back. My husband drives on slowly and with extreme care, barely talking, eyes focused on the track ahead. I lapse into silence in the cab, surprised at his carelessness but trying not to be.

The ocean's salty smell grows stronger as we swirl through sand drifts flowing across the track in graceful waves, ford a tidal waterway called Duck Creek, and drive along a beach with waves lapping at the wheels. Yes, waves!

'This is Jago's beach. Brian's shack's up there,' Peter tells me, pointing into the darkness. 'He's not here at the moment. Last week he gave me a fresh crayfish.'

'Delicious?'

'Best I've ever eaten.'

The headlights momentarily light up more piles of giant brown spaghetti off to the side. I sit as far forward on my seat as I can. My blood is surging through my veins and I'm craning my neck to see through the darkness, wanting to take in everything all at once and right now. In my excitement, I push away the anxiety that hovers at the back of my mind, for this track is our only road to town.

Further on, the headlights shine on a long, black mud puddle that looks like spilt treacle.

'Hold on,' my husband yells.

I grab the dashboard as our momentum abruptly slows. With the engine revving and the wheels spinning, the Land Rover inches forward through the mud for long seconds. We reach the other end of the mud and the tyres grip the firm ground and heave us out of the treacle. In the glow of the headlights, Peter turns to me and grins in relief. A few metres further on, he stops the vehicle and takes a pouch of tobacco out of his top pocket and rolls a cigarette.

Soon we're bowling along on hard-packed sand. Bracken fern fronds brush the sides of the cab. At the top of a gully, the headlights shine down onto a bridge, a crazy, sloping, timber bridge that drags one side in the water, like a bird with a broken wing. The creek flows beneath the timber decking on the upstream side but emerges in the middle of the structure.

'George Town Packet Creek,' Peter says. 'There hasn't been much rain lately, so we don't need the bridge anyway. We'll ford the creek.'

Water surrounds the Land Rover as it takes us through the creek with ease, although the noise of the engine in the cab is louder than ever. As we climb out on the other side, the vehicle sheds water like a submarine. We roar up the steep bank with a surge of power from the engine that's matched by a surge of exhilaration deep in my body. I feel vitally alive and fully in the moment, filled up to the brim with the thrill of this extraordinary journey.

Soon there's another creek with another timber bridge, level this time, which bangs and crashes as we drive across.

'Squatters Creek,' my husband says.

'How did these creeks get their names? Do you know?'

'No.'

The headlights surprise an owl into flight and later startle a dark shadow in the middle of the track.

'A Tasmanian devil. Don't confuse the devil with the Tasmanian tiger – that's the rare one,' he tells me. 'There're lots of devils on the farm and they eat anything. One even nibbled Bob's leather boots. He'd left them in the shed overnight and came out next morning to find a hole in one of the heels. Mad as a cut snake, he was. They were good boots.'

I remember the talk in Schultzie's shack about Tasmanian devils becoming bolder. I can't wait to see one of these creatures close up.

Soon we're climbing a steep slope of dried mud, hard runnels of caked dirt criss-crossing each other.

'This is the last hill before the farm,' my husband shouts above the noise of the engine labouring under the strain. 'Just as well there's been no rain, otherwise Bob'd have to tow us up with the tractor.'

Not knowing what he meant, and not at that moment wanting to know, I sit on the edge of my seat and stare at the wheel ruts leading the vehicle upwards.

Three hours after leaving Zeehan, we bounce through an open gate and drive over a grassy paddock. Ahead there are two rectangles of yellow light in the darkness. The house. We enter a yard and pull up at the front. The door opens and out jumps our partner, Bob.

Yes, jumps. There don't appear to be any steps.

# 2

## His tail was on fire

'Joanna. Here you are at last. Pete'll be happy. He's been behaving like a bear with a sore head.'

'Anyone would, living with you, Werner,' my husband says, grinning, and slapping his friend on the shoulder before unloading cartons of groceries and my suitcases from the back of the vehicle.

Bob encloses me in a bear hug. The wool of his jumper is rough on my cheek. He's an affectionate man and I know his welcome is genuine. I follow him up three steep metal steps, like a short ship's ladder, and through the front door into an alcove. Gumboots and rifles stand against the walls and raincoats hang on hooks. Packets of bullets, jars of nails and bottles of kerosene sit on a high shelf. The alcove leads into a closed-in veranda that runs the length of the cottage. There's no internal lining in the veranda so spiders and insects have made their homes on the exposed skeleton of the house. Dusty cobwebs swing from diagonal timbers. Bridles, saddles and a carton of old magazines litter the floor. I see two small circular holes in a window, and stop. Bullet holes? A new gas stove and refrigerator sparkle with whiteness on a raised platform.

The bare floorboards creak under my weight as I step into the main room. There are two easy chairs, a coffee table with a chessboard set into its top, a packing case covered with a fringed tartan rug and a kerosene heater which gives its smell to the room. Two calendars with curling corners hang on the walls, one with a photograph of a naked blonde woman, the other advertising fertiliser. A bookcase is crammed with agricultural pamphlets, rolled-up maps, a compass and shells.

A bench along one wall is the 'kitchen'. There's a blue plastic bowl on top and a cupboard underneath. Peter has warned me there's no plumbing in the house. Water has to be carried inside in buckets from a rainwater tank behind the dwelling.

The lack of plumbing leaves a lot to be desired, but the room is lit by an electric light bulb hanging from the ceiling. I give thanks for the electricity supplied by a three-kva diesel generator, throbbing away in a shed outside. Peter has already told me that he and Bob bought the generator and installed it on a cement base in the main shed, but to see electric lights in the house with my own eyes brings civilisation closer.

Leaning against the end wall of the living room is a sheet of rusty corrugated iron which screeches as I pull it away and peer behind. I see grass and feel cold air on my face. Ah. A gap in the wall for a fireplace.

I walk into the bedroom, which is also lit by a light bulb suspended from the ceiling. A double bed with a dark wooden headboard is made up with clean sheets and blankets. I smile to myself, glad my husband has his priorities right.

Peter comes in with my suitcases. We hug and talk happily, but later, as I stand in the living room and gaze at the unpainted walls, the frayed fabric of the lounge chairs and the 'kitchen' on the benchtop, my chest tightens with dismay. I plonk down on the makeshift sofa. Its sharp front edge digs into the backs of my knees through the thin rug. I try to recall my excitement at the idea of living on the wild west coast of Tasmania and my vow to throw myself into everything on Top Farm. So easy to say in the comfort of my parents' home in Canberra.

I sigh and climb to my feet, remembering that the landscape, the animals and the men I met at Granville have already sparked my interest. As for this cottage – we have everything we need for daily life. A roof over our heads, a bed to sleep in and, tucked into a pocket of my suitcase, a recipe for making bread.

*

I met Peter in Port Moresby in PNG, where I was working as a publications officer in the Education Department and he was a lands settlement officer in the Lands Department. Together we travelled through Mexico, Central America, Peru and Bolivia. In Mexico, we learned how to drink tequila – with lemon and salt and never to be repeated. In Peru, we marvelled at the ingenuity of the Incas, who built a fully functioning city on top of a remote mountain ridge, and in Bolivia, we visited a ski resort at the impossible altitude of five thousand four hundred metres.

At the end of our trip, we parted in Buenos Aires airport, a vast impersonal place with hundreds of hurrying people, too many loudspeakers and a metallic smell in the air. After a final kiss, we boarded our different planes. He returned to PNG. I flew on to the United Kingdom and Europe. Some time later, I returned to Australia and married him – 'after her money ran out', he quipped to friends years later.

After our wedding in Canberra in March 1973, we flew back to PNG and lived and worked in Popondetta. Independence was looming for the country and we wanted to make the move to Australia. Our friend Bob Werner made a wild suggestion. A cattle property on the west coast of Tasmania was for sale. What about going into partnership?

Bob was older than us and had a supposedly shady past. Peter's parents, Phyl and George Barrett, warned us against him, but we were undeterred. A German with a hooked nose and an expressive face, he was energetic and intelligent and Peter and I were sure that together we'd turn the farm into a thriving cattle enterprise.

\*

Sunbeams shine through the bedroom window next morning and wake us. When I step outside, I find the air is warm and the sky is blue without a cloud, which I take for granted then. A fence surrounds the cottage and two small sheds. One of the sheds contains the toilet, a large can topped with a yellow toilet seat. I learn that the can has to be emptied when one can no longer sit without being tickled.

The other shed has weatherboard walls, a roof of corrugated iron and a weird-looking chimney at one end made up of pieces of corrugated iron fastened together and pointing crookedly to the sky. Peter and Bob store bags of fertiliser inside, stacked to shoulder height. Today they're loading bags onto the Land Rover, backed up to the door. Later, the fertiliser will be tipped into a spreader attached to the back of the tractor.

Ramshackle and dilapidated, the structure intrigues me. I know our partner worked on the west coast some years before. 'Did people live in this shed in the past, Bob?' I ask, as I rub my fingertips over the rough timber wall of the building.

He's standing on the back of the vehicle, and nods. 'Years ago it was the railway station master's office in Zeehan.'

My eyebrows shoot up in astonishment. 'How did it get here?'

He grunts as he takes a heavy bag from Peter and sets it down on the back of the Land Rover. 'Some blokes towed it out to use as the farm workers' camp. Probably when they were clearing the forest for pasture.'

'When was that?'

'Around sixty years ago. Maybe more. The men would've done everything in here. Eat, sleep, have smoko. Games of cards on wet days, too.'

I step inside and breathe in the smell of dust and old fires. The frameworks of four timber bunks are covered with chicken wire. Cobwebs hang from the walls and layers of dust cover every surface. I bend down at the fireplace and push the debris around with my fingertip. Puffs of ash rise up, together with a smell of smoke and old tobacco. A blackened tin can is all that remains in the fireplace but a thrill of excitement pulses through me. I've always loved places with history, hidden stories of lives lived in the past, and here is raw history at my fingertips.

I'm also astonished to learn that Zeehan had once had a railway. The town had been much bigger in the late 1800s and early 1900s than it is now, thanks to rich deposits of silver-lead, zinc and tin in the district, but I didn't know there'd been a railway linking it to other places. More history to learn about. My mind thrills at the prospect.

\*

Beyond the fence around the yard stands a large, red, corrugated-iron shed. I walk in and see the tractor, shelves of tools, workbenches and the diesel generator which gives us electricity.

Back outside, I look inland at the undulating paddocks which dip here and there into wooded gullies. A line of tall trees hides shadows along a creek. I sense mysteries among the shadows and feel the urge to explore.

A bird flies through my line of sight and vanishes into a stand of trees behind the fertiliser shed. A cacophony of squabbling erupts. I run to the trees and try to see the birds, but they're silhouettes against the sky.

Originally, the rich chocolate soil of Top Farm supported temperate rainforest, but, after the trees were cut down, the farm fattened cattle to feed thousands of miners trying their luck in the rugged west coast mountains and on the plains. Drovers on horseback walked the animals overland from the north coast, swimming them across the Arthur and Pieman Rivers on the way and walking them along Four Mile Beach. They were driven up onto Top Farm or further on to the Bottom Farm. I'm eager to find out more about this colourful history of the area.

Top Farm has been neglected for a long time. As I walk over the paddocks on my first day, I push through patches of bracken fern and fireweed. Stands of dogwood trees have reclaimed the edges of paddocks. Dogwoods are also known as cabbage musk, small trees that are slender and smooth-barked with raggedy leaves.

The house nestles into the eastern or inland side of the hill we'd climbed in the vehicle the evening before. I walk up to the top of the hill and gaze seawards. A breeze touches my cheek, bringing with it whiffs of sea salt. The ocean is calm and smooth and vast, as though a gentle giant has flung his royal blue cape to the far horizon. Separated from the farm by over a kilometre of stunted trees, swamps, sand dunes and even patches of quicksand, Four Mile Beach and its rocky outcrops beckon.

Most of the time, our partner lives with his wife, Annalies, at Oldina on the north coast. When Bob's on the farm, he stays in a caravan behind the cottage. He and Annalies left Germany and migrated to Australia after World War Two. He worked in Tasmania and in the Lands Department in PNG, where he was Peter's superior officer in the lands settlement section. The two became good friends; both were intelligent and quick-witted with a mischievous sense of humour and a love of the bush.

Peter and Bob repair fences, slash pastures regularly to eradicate bracken fern and fireweed, sow clover and rye grass seed, and drive the tractor and spreader around the paddocks followed by a faint white cloud of fertiliser.

I get the household tasks done as fast as I can so I'm free to explore my new world. I sweep the floor, cook meals and wash up plates and saucepans in the large plastic bowl on the bench. I even wash clothes and our double sheets in the bowl, a task helped along by lots of angst and a blaring radio; there's nothing like 'Rock Around The Clock' to lighten the load.

Every bucket of water has to be carried inside from the tank outside and the only way to heat the water is on the stove. After squeezing soapy water through a sheet as best I can, I wring out the surplus water and then drop it into a bucket of clean water at my feet to be rinsed. When the sheets and clothes are clean, I lug them outside to a rope slung between two trees to dry.

I'd known our living conditions would be rough, but I've already been captivated by my new life. I've loved the Australian bush since I was a little girl. My father, Yang (a name I called him ever since babyhood), was in the Royal Australian Air Force and for a time we lived on the RAAF base at Garbutt in Townsville, where he was the commanding officer of No. 10 Maritime Reconnaissance Squadron. Mum, Yang and I often packed picnic food into Bee Bee, our Standard car that was green with a canvas roof, and headed out into the country. Crystal Creek was a favourite spot, a creek with a rocky swimming hole in which the water was so deep we could jump off the cliff on the other side, and so clear we could see down to tiny pebbles on the bottom. At lunchtime, we cooked lamb chops over a fire and ate them with white bread and butter and tomato sauce. Delicious.

After Townsville, Yang was posted to Nowra Hill in New South Wales, where he was the air director at the Australian Joint Anti-Submarine School. The street in which we lived backed onto eucalypt forest and there were children in every house. After school and at weekends, we'd play skipping games on the road, catch tadpoles in the creek and build cubbies in the bush.

A water pipe spanning a gully formed a 'bridge'. With our legs straddling the pipe and our hands in front, feeling daring and brave, we'd inch our way across the rounded surface, trying not to look down to the bottom of the gully way below where scattered beams of sunlight slanted down onto lank grass. Afraid of falling yet loving the exhilaration, I'd reach the other end of the pipe and step off, grinning with glee. Then do it all over again.

During a later posting, we lived in Canberra. On weekends, Mum, Yang and I headed over the hills to the Brindabella River for picnics. Yang fished for trout and Mum and I swam in the clean, clear water, the surface of which reflected saplings and reeds growing on the banks. Smooth stones and pebbles on the river bed were coloured beige and apricot and deep charcoal grey.

My parents sowed the seeds of my love of the bush, but I bet they never dreamt I'd end up at the end of the world.

\*

With a bounce in my step, I set off from the house whenever I can and tramp all over the property. I squat down on my haunches and peer along game trails in thickets of bracken fern, imagining devils, wombats and pademelons moving through the tunnels at night. I breathe in the fresh, wild fragrance of dogwood trees, fireweed and bracken fern. The dogwoods are so close together that I scrape my jeans on the trunks as I squeeze between them. Skylarks skim over the paddocks and I laugh when native hens spy me and bolt to the nearest vegetation, their tails jerking up and down and their legs a blur.

I step into the temperate rainforest and breathe in the rich scent of sassafras, myrtle and blackwood trees. The forest is hushed yet pulses with life, and birds call high in the canopy. Mighty trees, anchored in the earth, stretch up to the sky. Tree trunks and the forest floor are festooned with luxuriant mosses and lichens, and many colourful fungi catch my eye. A thick carpet of fallen leaves muffles my footsteps. Giant tree ferns grow out of the tops of slender stumps, silent worshippers in a vast cathedral. I cannot guess that a year later we'll destroy parts of the rainforest in a desperate attempt to make money.

In the southern part of Top Farm there's a hilly paddock that slopes down to two dams, one above the other, linked by a tiny waterfall; we call them the 'double dams'. In the north, a ridge of pasture leads to the stockyards, horizontal trunks of gum trees forming a large square with corner posts, and two internal fences. The yards have never been finished and require more internal fencing, a holding yard, gates, a race and a bail before they can be used. More work for the men.

Near the northern boundary, a narrow, uneven track winds through stands of dogwood trees to Newdegate Creek. The rough track previously forded the creek and ascended a steep, forested hill to make its way to the 'old farm', an area cleared many years before by a man named McGuinness but now covered with two-metre-high bracken fern.

Like all west coast creeks, Newdegate is the colour of weak black tea, the water stained by tannin from buttongrass plains and tea tree vegetation upstream. This doesn't spoil its beauty. Shallow water ripples over stones and pebbles on the creek bed, while overhanging leatherwood and myrtle trees cast shadows on the surface. Ferns and reeds grow at the water's edge. Driftwood logs of deep grey, weathered logs washed downstream in a previous flood, lie strewn over the rapids. Newdegate Creek becomes one of my favourite places.

*

Peter takes me to Four Mile Beach. Thick bushes scratch the sides of the vehicle as the Land Rover bounces down a sandy track onto the southern end of the beach, which opens out in front of us. I draw in my breath at its vastness. I've never seen such a beach. Wild and windswept, with crashing waves on one side and towering sand dunes on the other, the beach stretches northwards and becomes lost in haze. The air is heavy with salt. I sense mysteries among the debris and can't wait to explore.

Waves crash onto wet sand and race up to meet me. I dip my hand into the water but snatch it back. The ocean is as cold as a melted iceberg.

This is my first visit to Four Mile Beach, although Peter has been here before. A chilly wind is blowing and I'm glad I've worn the llama-wool poncho I bought in Peru. In colours of chocolate, beige and cream with a fluffy fringe around the neck and hem, the poncho had kept me warm in the freezing temperatures of the Andes mountains.

'It's cold,' I say to Peter, snuggling into the poncho's warmth as he puts his arm around me. 'So cold.'

'Yeah, freezing all right,' he says, nodding.

Shells, tangles of dried seaweed and pieces of driftwood show tide levels on the dry sand. Some of the driftwood is so sun-bleached and weathered it resembles animal bones. Further back, sand dunes are piled upon sand dunes, and hardy plants eke out a living in sheltered spots. Several slopes are covered with the triangular, fleshy leaves of pigface. The delicate, daisy-like flowers that dot the trailing leaves seem out of place in this harsh environment.

We climb back into the vehicle and drive further along the beach. The northern end ahead is hidden by mist. Four miles is the length of this beach, its name tells me, yet I doubt if anyone has ever measured it. How does one measure vastness? With eons of time and a tape measure?

Peter drives on the firm wet sand but veers inland to avoid each wave. Ahead we see a creek flowing across the beach into the ocean. Miniature sand cliffs about thirty centimetres high show the banks. We check these on foot before fording the creek. Soon afterwards, we stop the Land Rover again and, in a carefree mood, explore our surroundings. Dainty little birds run ahead of us on the wet sand while larger seabirds wheel noisily in flight over an outcrop of rocks at the water's edge.

Debris at the tidemarks includes huon pine logs that began their lives many hundreds of years before as seedlings in an ancient forest. I feel awed by the magnificence of pristine nature – until I trip over a glass bottle half buried in the sand. We unscrew the top and sniff. Whisky. Soon we notice other rubbish washed up by the ocean tides. A plastic salt container, orange boxes, plastic buoys and even a length of yellow nylon rope, which my husband slings over his shoulder to take home.

He walks off to take a closer look at several trunks of huon pine he'd noticed during a previous trip to the beach. The logs had been thrown up to the base of a sand dune during past storms. He hopes to find one suitable to 'slice' with the chainsaw to make a coffee table.

I roam happily among the debris along the tide lines. Planning to make a sculptural still life, I gather small pieces of driftwood, dried ocean sponges, balls of tangled seaweed and shells. There are so many shells! Large saucer-shaped shells glowing with mother-of-pearl interiors (later I learn these are abalone); blue cones; mussels; and many others of varying shapes and sizes and colours. Wishing I'd brought a bucket for my treasures, I stuff them into the pockets of my jeans.

I lick my lips and taste the salt that's dried on my skin.

Scuffing the sand with my shoes, I work my way closer to the dunes at the back of the beach. There's a hillock of weathered, sun-bleached animal bones and shells partly covered by sand. I stop moving and hold my breath. After a long moment, I crouch down and study the pieces closely. Excitement races through me. It's a midden, an Aboriginal rubbish heap.

The sun is warm on my back and the air around me is utterly still as my mind races on. Over a hundred and forty years must have passed since the last bones and shells were tossed onto the midden. I pick up a small bone. It's white and pitted with tiny holes. I'm aware with a kind of awe that an Indigenous man or woman or even a child had long ago eaten the flesh from the bone that now lies in the palm of my hand.

The evening before, I'd begun reading a book Mum had given me about the last Tasmanian Aboriginal, Truganini.[1] Indigenous people had roamed the island freely until the white men arrived in the early 1800s and changed everything. I had become so absorbed in the book that I didn't want to put it down when Peter suggested it was time to turn off the generator and go to bed.

Now, standing on the beach and thinking about the words I'd read, I place the old bone back on the midden where it belongs and imagine the scene here all those years before.

Sitting in their windbreaks of bark laid against sticks driven into the sandy ground, the men are carving new waddies from short pieces of wood. A waddy is a wooden club, notched towards the grasp and slightly rounded at the point. The men's woolly hair and beards appear dull beside the shiny dark skin of their faces, skin which glistens as they work and talk.

Some members of the tribe wear kangaroo or possum skins, fastened over one shoulder, for warmth. There's a young mother who has no animal skin but whose shoulders and neck are decorated with a pattern of scars. Wearing a necklace of small iridescent shells strung together which tinkle as she moves, she has small hands and wide, splayed feet. As she works she keeps an eye on her baby sitting on the sand. An old woman is making a drinking vessel from leaves of kelp fashioned at each end. A wallaby speared that morning is roasting on a fire and I smell the hot, meaty fragrance in the air. I turn seawards, where women are gathering shellfish at a rocky outcrop near the water's edge. They place the shellfish in woven grass baskets while their children play and run –

A clod of wet sand hits my arm. I spin around, snapping out of my reverie. Peter is standing nearby holding a green glass sphere covered with rope woven in a diamond pattern. Spotlessly clean and gleaming from the action of sand and sea, the sphere shines in the sunlight.

'What about this as a lampshade base?' he says, beaming with pleasure.

*

Laden with our loot, we return to the vehicle. That afternoon I stand at the kitchen bench and fashion an oceanic still life using my treasures from the beach. A curling length of driftwood about twenty centimetres long becomes the vertical centrepiece, giving height to an arrangement of pebbles, seaweed, shells, smaller pieces of driftwood and ocean sponges. My composition is beginning to take on a pleasing shape when Peter comes into the house, his face glowing from the cold air outside.

I take away one of the shells in the still life and replace it with a cylindrical sponge, propping up the sponge with pebbles. 'Hi,' I say, low key.

He stands behind me and, slipping his arms around my waist, kisses my neck. 'Like to go to the beach again soon?'

'Umm,' I mumble as I rearrange the sponges and shells and driftwood. I like the smoothness of the shells, the grittiness of the seaweed and the timbery surface of the driftwood, and I like the salty fragrance of the sea the objects give to the air in the room.

I stand back and study my still life with a creative eye. I move a small piece of driftwood and gaze at the arrangement again, aiming for a pleasing combination of shape and colour and texture.

I realise my husband has disappeared. I realise something else, too. I love being absorbed in creative endeavours and on Top Farm I can do just that.

\*

Four Mile Beach is raw and vast and wild, and its wildness reaches deep into me. I've always loved remote places, where human concerns cease to exist. Here, it seems, nothing has changed for thousands of years, nothing, that is, except the ever-changing sea and its habit of throwing timber, seaweed, shells and ships' rubbish high up onto the sand.

Four Mile Beach always seems untouched, even though I know that humans have been visiting its windswept expanses for thousands of years. I'm only a speck on that beach, yet I feel immeasurably bigger for being there. I'm connected with the cosmos and part of it. I feel sure it will tell me the secrets of Nature, if only I will open my ears and listen. Its vastness reaches into me, into a primal place where I am an ancient myself, with an ancient's awe at his world and its mysteries.

Often, Four Mile Beach is a wild place where the sound of the wind fills my ears, drowning out all other sounds except the harsh cries of seabirds. It whips my hair into my face and stings my skin with sand particles. I breathe in the raw saltiness of the great ocean beyond the waves with profound pleasure, revelling in the grandeur and power of Nature all around.

At other times, the beach is as gentle as a soft summer's day, with warm sand underfoot, waves no higher than ripples in a creek and dainty birds chasing fairy-like crabs.

\*

Two horses belonging to the Casey brothers are agisted on Top Farm. Big Mick and Pinto are black and white stock horses and they often tear across the paddocks in a mad gallop.

One afternoon soon after I arrive, a low rumbling sound reaches my ears. The horses appear over the crest of a far hill and race towards the house with manes and tails streaming. The ground vibrates as they hurtle past twenty metres from the fence then wheel around and pull up. I reach out to Big Mick and let him smell my hand but when I try to pat him, he snorts and tosses his head. The smaller horse, Pinto, snorts and backs away, too.

I'd been riding on a relative's property near Canberra as a teenager and later at a riding school in Port Moresby. Gung-ho, I reckon I can ride Big Mick. If I'd stopped to think, I would have realised the well-trained, gentle mounts I'd previously ridden prepared me for Big Mick as well as flying a Cessna would prepare a pilot for a 747.

As soon as I settle into the saddle, Big Mick takes off. He's a part-Clydesdale stock horse, many hands high, as strong as an ox and accustomed to tough love. He accelerates into a gallop with his head low. My heart thrashes in my chest. The wind whips my face as we tear up the hill behind the house then fly down the other side, which is so steep I begin to slip forwards over his neck. Terror rises in my body. Holding my breath and tensing every muscle, I pull back as hard as I can on the reins but I might as well have been a fly on his back for all the notice Big Mick takes. He goes hell for leather as though his tail is on fire. Near the stockyards, he swings around and we head back the way we've come. All I can hear is the wind rushing past my ears. All I can think is *I've got to stay on.* I grip the reins with tight hands and press my thighs into the speeding creature's body as his hooves thunder over the ground. At the double dams, he turns a tight circle and we race back to the shed, where he stops so abruptly I fall off.

'Enjoy the ride?' Peter asks with a wicked grin as he takes the reins.

I'm too shaken to think of a retort for my ever-loving husband. I lean against the wall until I can breathe again. Big Mick is quiet and contented now, nibbling the grass and swishing his tail.

I'm so relieved to be in one piece that it isn't until later, nursing a cup of tea in the house, that I laugh at myself. Silly girl. Fancy thinking I could ride a strong stock horse like Big Mick!

Nevertheless, as I drain the last of my tea, I vow to redeem myself somehow, sometime in the future.

# 3

# Putting down roots

By now we're starting to stock the property with cattle. Bob goes to stock sales in Burnie, a big town on the north coast, and purchases Hereford heifers, Murray grey cows with calves, Hereford steers and two Hereford bulls. Our aim is to build up a herd of high-quality cows whose heifers join the breeding herd and whose male calves are castrated and, in time, sold as prime beef.

The animals are trucked to Granville Harbour. The men meet the truck there, offload the animals and walk them along the track to Top Farm, a walk that takes several hours.

I watch the newcomers as they reach our sweet grass. The heifers and steers kick their heels and gambol over the paddocks, while the more sedate cows and bulls amble over the grass and lower their heads to begin grazing.

Still and relaxed, I stand in the paddock. Cattle have a strong streak of curiosity and I hope that the animals will investigate. Several cows walk towards me with eyes alert and tails swinging. One comes closer until she's standing about three metres away. Lifting her nose, she sniffs the air and looks at me with deep, dark eyes. Her eyes are like mulled wine and I stare into their depths and, in that moment, I fall in love with cows. There's wisdom in those eyes and knowledge of the seasons and how to rear youngsters. I know I'm being fanciful, yet I can't look away. I speak to her softly and she swings her head to one side, her eyes never leaving my face. She steps closer and extends her head. I lift my hand towards the wet rubber of her nose but she jumps backwards, crashing her hooves on the ground. Soon, she approaches me again, her eyes watching me with wary interest. This time, she sniffs my hand before turning away. A thrill surges through me.

The men count the animals. Two calves are mooing in distress and the count confirms that two cows are missing.

'They've probably gone off into the bush at Duck Creek,' Peter says.

He and Bob fit the calf crate, an open-topped wire crate, on to the back of the Land Rover, and load the calves into it. They drive to Duck Creek, where the young animals' bellowing brings their mothers trotting out of the bush. Eagerly, the two cows follow the vehicle along the track and up to Top Farm, their full udders swinging from side to side.

Two Hereford steers are missing, too. Peter reckons they probably panicked at Granville and galloped away from the mob and into the bush. I can't blame them. After the gentle meadows of Tasmania's north coast, they would have smelled the salt in the air at Granville and heard the surf crashing onto the rocks with terror.

'They'll find their way to the paddocks on the Bottom Farm,' Bob reckons.

Peter agrees.

'Coming, Jo?' Bob asks me early the next morning.

We're standing outside the shed. The calf crate is still on the back of the Land Rover, and Peter and Bob are about to set off.

I stare at them as the penny drops. 'You're going to bring the steers back on the vehicle?' Although only yearlings, Hereford steers stand as high as cows and are as leggy as young teenagers. 'It'll be top-heavy and tip over in the first uneven wheel rut.'

'Nothing to worry about,' Bob says. 'We won't tip over.' He shrugs and adds, 'Even if we do, we'll be going so slowly no one will be hurt.'

My mouth falls open.

'The worst thing that could happen is the crate could burst apart and the animals'd escape again.'

I close my mouth and stare at him, unconvinced. 'How much do two steers weigh?'

'About a thousand kilos altogether,' Peter puts in.

My brain warns me this will be a drama-filled trip and my heart beats faster in my chest. I'm back on that pipe in the bush at Nowra Hill, exhilarated to be inching my way across, yet afraid of falling into the gully way below. That addictive mixture of exhilaration and fear.

'I'm coming.' I run inside and grab my sunglasses.

We trundle southwards along the track, drive through Granville and reach the gate to the Bottom Farm. Peter pops out and opens the gate. A well-maintained track takes us through undulating green pastures neatly fenced and descending here and there to wooded gullies. There are bush belts of blackwood and myrtle trees. Cattle dot the paddocks.

Bottom Farm cattle are sold regularly at north-west coast stock sales. It's the first time I've been on the property and I know it shows the potential of our place. Looking at the green grass and healthy cattle, I feel reassured about our future on Top Farm.

Don Smith's wife, Lois, is staying at the farm for a few days with her two young children. I'm thrilled to meet her. While the men go off to load the steers into the crate on the Land Rover – our two wayward Herefords did, indeed, find their way to the Bottom Farm, and Jim and Don put them into their stockyards – Lois greets me warmly and invites me into their cosy home. Dressed in slacks and an olive-green shirt, she has pretty brown hair which falls in waves around her face. The baby on her hip stares at me with big eyes.

Lois puts on the kettle and makes coffee, then feeds baby Megan silverbeet with a spoon. Bob had told me Lois had grown up on a farm near Devonport, so I'm intrigued to know why this farmer's wife has chosen town life now that she has her own family.

'I don't want to live out here. It's too isolated,' she says, pausing to wipe silverbeet from her daughter's pink cheeks with a washer. 'I come out with the children for a few days every so often. Royce is four and he loves being on the farm with Don. He follows the cattle around and has rides on Don's horse, Pedro. But it's too far to take the children into school when they're older. And if we need a doctor in a hurry, we have to drive all the way to Zeehan.'

I sip my coffee and think about our isolation on Top Farm in relation to children.

'No, I'll stop in town, thanks,' Lois declares. 'What about you, Jo?'

'I love it out here,' I say without hesitation, at the same time admiring Lois for knowing her own mind. Wishing to be polite, I add, 'When it comes to having young children, it's a different matter, I guess.' Even as I speak, I think of the thousands of isolated rural families in outback Australia. I may be the only woman who's lived on Top Farm, but I'm hardly unique.

We hear the sound of the Land Rover pulling up outside. I gasp when I see the Hereford steers in the crate. Their heads top the roof of the cab and they stare at us with wide, terror-filled eyes.

We set off and bump along the track with the vehicle rocking from side to side like a top-heavy ship. The steers bellow their distress and continually scrabble for hoof-holds on the back of the vehicle, banging against the sides of the crate. I sit in the middle of the cab with Bob driving and Peter on my left. We drive through Granville then come to the first bad section of the track, two uneven wheel ruts running along the rocky shore. Packed sand, embedded rocks and loose stones make up the track and we continually lean over, first to one side then to the other. The engine roars and the steers bellow as we drive up a steep, rock-strewn slope, leaning to the left, then further to the left as a half-buried boulder in the right-hand rut rises beneath the wheels. The steers slide to the left-hand side of the crate and the vehicle leans over even more. The saliva in my mouth dries up and I hold my breath. Bob begins whistling. The crate creaks and the engine groans with the strain. Bob's whistling grows louder and faster. We lean so far over that I fall onto Peter.

Slowly, ever so slowly, the vehicle rights itself as the wheel ruts even out beyond the boulder. I breathe out and the tension in my body eases, but the thrill of the trip stays with me as we trundle along the track, continually swaying from side to side. It reminds me of the day I'd picked my way across a swaying, cane footbridge over a river in a remote village in Papua a couple of years before, where Peter and I were on an election patrol. The bridge spanned rushing water three metres below and swayed from side to side as I moved my feet one at a time along the flimsy 'decking', composed of lengths of cane lashed together. I clung to the rope rails and tried to keep my balance, swaying all the time, my heart in my mouth. I breathed out in relief when I stepped off at the other end, but that afternoon, when we had to return the same way, I walked onto the footbridge with no hesitation, and enjoyed the exhilarating mixture of fear and excitement as I swayed from side to side.

*

The swaying of the Land Rover doesn't bother my companions. They're as relaxed as if they're heading to a corner shop for a bottle of milk and a newspaper. Talk about electric fencing fills the cab, and whether or not it'd be suitable for some of our paddocks.

We swirl through a sand drift across the track, before a familiar thirty-metre-long, black mudhole looms ahead. The mud is thick and sticky, like treacle in cold weather. If the vehicle gets bogged in the treacle, we'll have to let the steers go in order to lighten the load and dig the vehicle out.

Whistling again, Bob drives into the mudhole with a good balance of forward momentum and revs. The wheels begin to spin. Jets of mud spatter the underside of the Land Rover so hard, I can hear them above the noise of the engine. Crawling forward, wheels spinning, we lean way over to the left. No one speaks. The poor steers moo and roar on the back but the vehicle keeps moving forwards, helped by their weight, which gives the wheels some traction. Eventually, the tyres grip the dry surface of the track beyond the mudhole. Relieved, Peter rolls a cigarette and Bob stops whistling. They resume their discussion about electric fencing.

The approach to George Town Packet Creek is steep with a ninety-degree turn halfway down. On the inside of the angle there's a ditch between the track and an overhanging sand bank covered in bracken fern and saplings. As we drive slowly down the slope and turn the corner at the ninety-degree turn, the vehicle tips so far over the ditch towards the sand bank that the tops of the bracken brush the crate. My heart thrashes in my chest as I fall onto Peter again, yet we don't tip over.

I feel certain we've defied gravity, but our passengers aren't impressed. When we reach the farm, the steers leap out of the crate as soon as it's opened and gallop to the furthest corner of the paddock.

Relieved the runaway steers are finally on Top Farm, we stand around the vehicle for a few minutes.

'There's steak in the fridge, Bob. Feel like cooking tonight?'

Our partner's eyes brighten and he nods.

That evening, we eat Bob's trademark meal of fillet steak flavoured with mustard and garlic, a tasty, tender dish accompanied by mashed potatoes and vegetables. Our conversations range from the Vietnam War, which is nearing its end, to the wisdom of PNG gaining independence from Australia, and on to World War Two. Bob had fought in World War Two – on the German side. He'd been a soldier in the Nazi army during the invasion of the Soviet Union in June 1941, a massive offensive that stalled on the outskirts of Moscow and became a war of attrition. Conditions for the soldiers were grim, especially during the following winter. Food was scarce, and clothing and blankets were in short supply. There was no rest for the soldiers.

'That's when I taught myself to catnap whenever I could,' Bob tells us that evening.

On Top Farm, his catnaps become part of the daily landscape and, on one occasion, contribute to a dramatic incident involving a runaway bulldozer.

※

Every day, there's housework to do. Like most cleaning, dusting is a thankless job, only noticed if it's not done. Our government house in Popondetta fronted a dirt road that sent its dust swirling inside every time a vehicle passed along, so I accepted ruefully that the louvres on every window would act as A1 dust collectors. Not only the louvres, of course. Every surface in every room became coated with dust.

Imagine my shock when I discover dust in the Top Farm cottage! How dare the dust gods inflict such a thing on the furniture and windowsills of a house surrounded by grassy paddocks!

I sigh to myself as I do the rounds with a feather duster and an old rag. I reach the inevitable conclusion that all houses, wherever they are, collect dust.

On a rare trip to Burnie, I buy knitting needles and wool; a teach-yourself-to-crochet book plus cotton and a crochet hook; bread-making ingredients and a big bowl; and four blankets and a duck-down doona. Peter and I also purchase every book about the west coast we can lay our hands on.

In wet weather, I read, write in my diary and pen long letters to friends. I also start to write for a newspaper in Tasmania. In PNG, I'd written articles that were published in magazines and newspapers, and there's plenty to write about on Top Farm. During that trip to Burnie, I'd visited the offices of *The Advocate* newspaper and, with the editor's encouragement, begin to write articles about Top Farm and the west coast.

In Burnie, I also buy paint: a tin of undercoat and a tin of forest green paint. During the following week, I paint the front door, after scraping off the pink paint that has adorned it for years and is flaking off in pieces the size of twenty-cent coins. As I apply the last coat with sweeping brushstrokes, with the smell of the paint in my nostrils and splotches of green on my hands and arms, I smile to myself with profound and secret pleasure. The green door gives the cottage charm and identity.

\*

My blithe declaration that I wanted to experience 'the full catastrophe' on Top Farm soon comes back to haunt me. One wet morning, Peter and Bob are building two timber bunk beds at one end of the closed-in veranda. I lean on the doorjamb, trying to help, while they saw and hammer, talk and banter. I hang around wanting to be useful but only getting in the way. Excluded from the male camaraderie, dejected and gloomy, I wonder what I'm doing on a remote farm at the end of the world. My limbs feel heavy and useless. I'm tempted to plonk down into a chair and stare at the wall, but instead I climb into a raincoat and rainhat and trudge along the ridge towards the stockyards, kicking tussocks of grass with the toe of my gumboot.

I lean my forehead against a grey timber rail wet with rain, shoving my hands deep into the pockets of my raincoat. The gentle drizzle falls on my shoulders, and my gumboots squelch in the mud as I shift my feet. I think about the men absorbed in their carpentry work back at the house, enjoying their male, workaday world.

All around me, drizzly mist covers the further landscape. Closer, my eyes find a grassy spot set among half a dozen trees at the edge of the paddock, where, a few nights earlier, Peter and I had startled a wombat. The creature had lumbered off with surprising speed and agility. Most of the native animals on Top Farm are nocturnal, so we often tramp over the paddocks in the evenings with a torch. I breathe in the fragrance of rain on rich grass and hear the call of a plover wheeling over the grass behind me.

These are pleasant thoughts but they don't help. I sigh. There's only one thing to do. I'll bake a batch of scones. As I stride back to the house, my mouth waters at the thought of eating hot scones with melting butter and strawberry jam. I watch the cattle grazing in the mist and think objectively about the situation. I can't be included in everything. And with bunk beds in the house, Peter's and my parents and our friends will be able to visit us, a thrilling thought.

What's more, the men will welcome a hot, tasty morning tea. Once again, I'll feel I belong in our little group.

\*

Donny Smith gives us an old cement laundry trough. Peter positions the trough outside the loo shed, along the lee wall. He lays a pipe from the water tank underground to the trough, and attaches a tap at the end. Washing sheets, jeans and jumpers in the trough is an enormous improvement on a bowl on the kitchen bench, but I look forward to the day when our twin-tub washing machine arrives from PNG, along with the rest of our household goods. For now, I simply get on with washing clothes the Top Farm way. I don't resent it and it isn't a burden; simply part of life.

Peter and I decorate the living room of our little home. This pleases me no end. We lay seagrass matting on the floor, hang curtains on the windows and tapa cloth from PNG on the wall. At a second-hand furniture shop in Zeehan, we buy a dining table and six matching blackwood chairs; we also buy a little desk which I position under the window in the bedroom. The living room takes on a homely air, especially on the days when I pick wildflowers in the bush and arrange them in a vase (a peanut butter jar) on the table.

On the top of the bookshelf, I place a pair of onyx bookends I'd bought in Mexico. Sandwiched between them are pamphlets and books about the west coast, novels we'd brought with us and the book about the last Tasmanian Aboriginal, Truganini. The onyx bookends are a creamy beige colour and each is a carving of a Mexican man asleep under his sombrero beside a tall cactus. I'd cursed those heavy onyx bookends that had weighed down my suitcase in Mexico in the days before I'd packed them off by seamail to Australia, but now I'm glad of their presence. I love my two Mexicans. They represent a time in my life when the adventure had been easy.

My handyman husband lines the internal walls of the veranda and we move the kitchen into there. Below the window, he installs a proper sink complete with a tap connected to a pipe which brings water from the tank outside. Kitchen cupboards with a bench on top go in against the wall opposite the sink. I paint the cupboards green, a lighter green than the front door. We acquire a meat safe, a small cupboard with a door and three shelves and gauze on the front and sides.

On the wall above the cupboards, Peter builds shelves where I keep casserole dishes and packets of dried herbs, and flour and rice in colourful pots. I cover the wall behind the bench with orange-and-green-patterned contact paper and we screw onto the wall our one and only mod-con, a mechanical tin opener. Beside the fridge there's a shelf where I keep recipe books and a plant called a wandering jew in a pot.

The kitchen is light and airy with a panoramic view through the window of the undulating paddocks of the property. During long car trips with my parents as a child, I'd spent many hours sitting in the back seat and staring out of the window at grassy paddocks, scattered gum trees and grazing stock. In a strange sort of way, I'm in a very familiar place.

With each improvement to the house, the sense of isolation fades further away. Zeehan is no closer and our road no better, but we're making a mark on the place, establishing ourselves more solidly and with greater comfort. I've fallen in love with cows and I love exploring the bush and the beach.

I'm putting down roots on Top Farm.

# 4

# An amateur archaeologist

During our first couple of weeks on Top Farm, we either shivered while we took a shower outside, under the eaves of the fertiliser shed where a canvas shower bucket hung from a hook, or made do with an APC (armpits and crutch) wash with a bucket of warm water inside. So imagine my delight when Peter sets up a nearly-proper shower in a little room at one end of the closed-in veranda. With a shower base on the floor, which is a waterproof square with raised edges and an outlet pipe, and a railing above head height holding a shower curtain, the cubicle is nearly complete. Add a canvas shower bucket suspended from a rope, and hey presto! There's our shower.

\*

One day, I heat water on the gas stove, pour it into a plastic bucket and carry it into the bathroom. There's a rope attached to the handle of the canvas shower bucket which is looped through a pulley suspended from the ceiling and tied to a hook screwed into the wall. I let down the canvas bucket, pour in the water, hoist it to the right height and tie the rope at the wall.

I undress quickly, shivering in the cool air; even in summer, the air is cool – this is Tasmania. There's an adjustable metal rose attached to the bottom of the canvas bucket. I spin it around to turn the water on. Hot water gushes out, caressing my face and my shoulders and the whole of my body. My flesh tingles with utter pleasure. It's a glorious feeling and I want to hug the water in gratitude.

After turning the rose down to a trickle, I soap myself all over.

The capacity of the canvas bucket is eighteen litres. It's not a lot of wet stuff, but it's enough to have a good wash, if you're efficient. Me? Efficient? I'm a daydreamer. I won't tell you how many times I get caught out and have to rinse off in cold water. Ugh!

\*

'You can't go wrong,' my PNG friend Jan had told me as she handed over her tried-and-true recipe for making bread.

With this daunting prediction in mind, I set about making my first loaf. I sift a pinch of salt with the flour, add yeast and sugar, and gradually add water to create a stodgy mixture. I flour my hands and work the dough for four or five minutes, breathing in the fragrance that rises into my nostrils. I put the dough into a bowl, cover it, and allow it to prove. Unable to resist taking a peek, I'm thrilled to see that the yeast is doing its job and the mixture is rising.

When the dough has doubled in size, I knock it down again and bash and squash it, then shape it and place it into a floured bread tin. I let the dough prove once again, then slip the tin into the oven, which I've preheated.

When I open the oven, the hot, moist aroma of freshly baked bread fills the kitchen. Using an oven cloth, I slide out the tin and plonk it onto the bench with a satisfying clunk. My mouth waters. Soon, I'll be tucking into a slice of hot bread with puddles of melting butter on the top. I upend the tin and turn out the bread onto the bread board. Using the bread knife, which has a serrated blade, I start to saw a slice off the loaf, or try to. The knife won't go into the loaf at all, it won't even grip the surface. Using all of my strength, I saw back and forth, but my heart sinks. The bread is so dense, I can't cut it.

I let out a heavy sigh.

Using the point of a sharp knife, I pierce the surface of my wooden bread, tuck my thumbs into the holes and wrestle the thing into two big pieces. I try to bite off a mouthful but it's too tough.

Dejected, I sink into a chair. So much for the 'can't go wrong' recipe.

Eventually, I manage to tear off a couple of pieces of wooden bread for the horses. Have you ever been rejected by a horse? Two horses? Big Mick and Pinto drop the bread onto the grass. They lift their heads and gaze at me, flicking their tails.

My second loaf of bread is even harder than the first.

'I'll bring in the chainsaw,' Peter quips.

I punch his arm and pretend to laugh, but my spirits sink further. Every man and his dog can bake bread, so why can't I?

Clearly what I lack is the knack.

Peter and I pore over the pictures in our bird book and learn the names of birds we see. White-faced herons visit the grass in our house yard. Plovers wheel over the paddocks. Every so often, a beautiful bird graces our pastures with its presence, feeding on prey which it digs up with its long curved bill. I'm thrilled when I identify it as a straw-necked ibis. Blue wrens nest in the vegetation near the house. Sometimes, I watch a scarlet robin from the kitchen window as it searches for insects among the grass in the yard, often, to my delight, perching on the top of a grass stalk and bending it over into a horseshoe shape.

There's something very satisfying about studying a bird in the wild and finding its exact picture in the book. Not that I'm always successful. Pipits (or were they skylarks?) swoop over the grass of the paddocks; it takes me a while to learn which is which.

One cold morning, a heavy mist hangs over the farm and the trees along the far creek are swathed in whiteness. Holding the egg-flip, I glance out of the kitchen window and notice half a dozen native hens pecking at the ground just on the other side of the fence. I put down the egg-flip, open the door quietly and begin to walk towards the birds, hoping to study them up close. I am still many metres away when they spy me and bolt to the creek, disappearing into the ghostly undergrowth with tail feathers bobbing up and down.

Currawongs, too, are frequent visitors. Large black birds up to fifty centimetres in length with shiny plumage, bright yellow eyes and massive bills, they forage noisily among the grass in the yard and peck worms from the moist soil. I start throwing small amounts of chopped meat onto the ground for these sharp-eyed creatures. As soon as I step back inside the house, they fly down and eat every piece. After a couple of days, they are feeding a couple of metres away from me and it isn't long before the bravest follows a trail of meat up to my hand and eats the pieces I'm holding.

I should have stopped then and there, because, in the following days, the birds hang around the door of the house like teenagers outside a café. One afternoon, the door is open and one of them flies inside, filling the kitchen with flapping wings and sinister, guttural noises. My heart pounds in panic. I'm trapped in an Alfred Hitchcock horror film.

'Shoo! Shoo!' Waving my arms wildly, I try to steer the creature towards the alcove and the door, but one of its wings slams into my forehead. Angry and indignant now, I shout at the invader. 'Get out before you poop in my kitchen,' but the panicking bird sees green grass through the window and crashes into the invisible wall.

It bounces back in shock and flaps towards me again, but this time I manage to guide it towards the alcove, where it lands on a high shelf. With wings beating harder than ever, it clings to a box of nails but the box falls off and crashes to the floor, scattering the contents and frightening the poor thing even more.

Eventually, I steer the creature out of the open door. The nails have fallen all over the place as well as into gumboots and buckets standing on the floor. I retrieve them one by one, cursing the currawong yet also feeling sorry for it. That poor bird had got more than it bargained for.

\*

One morning, I stroll out to the vegetable garden, open the gate and step in, and gasp with surprise and pleasure. Ten days earlier, I'd planted two rows of pea seeds. Now there are green shoots poking up through the dark chocolate soil, thrusting their tips to the sky. I squat down and gaze at the dark green seedlings that are already over a centimetre in length; there'd been no sign of them the day before. I put out my finger and touch one of the young plants. It's so strong that its surface resists my touch. I grin to myself, my heart swelling in my chest. From that moment, I am hooked on gardening.

We'd begun the vegetable garden by building a paling fence to keep out the wind, wallabies, horses and cattle. Soon, a fence of vertical saplings surrounds the garden area, which measures fourteen metres by seven metres. Peter borrows Brian Jago's rotary hoe and turns over the rich brown soil. To our surprise, he unearths many objects which fire up my curiosity. There must have been a shack on the spot some time before. Like an amateur archaeologist, I kneel down and poke in the soil with my fingers. I find old batteries, rusty tins, shards of broken glass and metal bolts. I examine everything I find, turning each object over in my fingers, as dirt gathers under my nails. The rich fragrance of the moist, dark soil fills my head. I spy something white half hidden in the earth. I dig with my fingers and uncover a piece of china. I pick it up, shake off the clinging earth, and gasp with excitement. Sitting on the palm of my hand is a delicate blue and white handle from a china cup. With my thumb, I rub the remaining dirt off the smooth, shiny surface and grin with pleasure.

We'd already learned from Bob that there'd been a shack on this spot which had burned down some time before. The shack was used by drovers bringing cattle down from the north coast, or by wallaby shooters out from Zeehan. What were these men doing with a fine china cup? Everyone on the west coast has told me I'm the first woman to live on Top Farm.

The sun falls on the china as it lies on my palm. The glazed surface shines and I wonder about its owner. Not a woman, I decide. Rather, a man who'd brought with him various things to use in his camp, including a china cup no longer wanted at home because it was chipped. Maybe the rest of the cup is buried in the soil? I dig and dig but it doesn't turn up. Nevertheless, I am thrilled with my find and the handle from the china cup becomes one of my treasures in the house.

\*

In the vegetable garden, there are six large beds with paths between them and narrow beds running around the inside of the fence. The peas are followed by tiny wispy carrots. Zucchini seeds explode into seedlings nearby, growing so fast I'm sure I can see the growth taking place before my eyes. We plant tomatoes, cabbages, Brussels sprouts, onions, beetroot, lettuces, potatoes, silverbeet and parsnips in between beds of flowers: cornflowers, carnations, poppies, foxgloves, pansies and marigolds. We plant raspberry canes and strawberry runners, covering the latter with wire netting to protect the fruit from birds. Among them all go parsley, chives, sage, thyme, fennel, garlic and mint. The mint wants to spread too much, so I transplant it into a pot sunk into the ground.

I water and weed and learn as I go with the help of a gardening book that Mum has given me. I tie the tomatoes to stakes and pinch off the lateral shoots. I thin out the lettuces and carrots, and dust the brassicas – cabbages, Brussels sprouts, cauliflowers and broccoli – to kill caterpillars. When the rhubarb is ready to cut, I learn from a cookbook how to prepare it. Not to stew the rhubarb stalks for hours until they become a watery tangle of purple string, but to poach them slowly in a small amount of sugared water. Previously, I'd scoffed at rhubarb pies, but change my mind when I bake a rhubarb pie to die for. We eat it hot with whipped cream.

The cauliflowers take months to mature. I part the top leaves and stare in at the baby white cauliflower growing within. Eventually, I decide one is ready to harvest. The plant is so big I need the largest kitchen knife to cut through the stem. Leaving the roots in the ground for the time being, I carry the cauliflower to the house but it's so huge I trip over the leaves. I slice them off and take the enormous head into the kitchen. I decide to make cauliflower soup. Using garlic and chicken stock, I simmer cauliflower pieces until they're tender. I push them through a sieve and add a little cream. That soup distills the very essence of cauliflower. I'd never known that cauliflowers could have such a rich flavour.

I spend hours gardening, totally absorbed in my world. If the weather is drizzly, I potter around in my raincoat and gumboots. One day, I'm absorbed in pushing long twigs as makeshift stakes into the soil around the latest planting of peas, when I hear a slight noise and look up to see Big Mick on the other side of the paling fence. He lowers his head over the palings and, with his big lips, plucks up the biggest fennel plant, pulling its roots out of the soil. I jump up and shout at him, but he ignores me, as usual. The plant dangles from his thick lips, its roots dropping soil.

I run over shouting, waving my arms in the air. 'Stop. Put it down.'

The big horse eyes me with contempt and starts to chew his prize, but abruptly steps back, tosses his head and spits it out. The aniseed flavour of fennel is apparently not to his liking.

'Ha. Serves you right.'

Fennel must be a hardy species because I replant this specimen and it grows into a flourishing bush that has to be cut back every year. In a cookbook, I find a recipe for fennel potato pie, a combination of bacon, potatoes and cheese sauce flavoured with fennel, which becomes a lunchtime favourite on cold days.

\*

My third attempt at bread making rises so much in the oven that it hits the roof and flows down the sides of the tin. I end up with an enormous loaf of bread that's hollow inside and an oven that has to be scraped clean. Big Mick eats the scrapings but Pinto spits them out and, backing away, eyes me with suspicion.

I groan and glare back at him. Pinto usually copies Big Mick. If the bigger horse decides to fly over the ground in a wild brumby gallop, Pinto gallops after him. If he refuses to be caught in the paddock, Pinto refuses also. If he rolls on the grass to wriggle and scratch, Pinto does the same.

The only time Pinto doesn't follow Big Mick's lead is in eating my bread.

Ouch. To be judged thus by a horse is a real slap in the face. I vow I will succeed in this bread-making caper, come what may.

*

One day as I walk along the side of the hill up to the farm, I see the entrance to a large burrow, a hole that's a metre in diameter. Excitement zips through my body. A wombat's burrow! One of these intriguing animals has started visiting our yard at night and I'm no doubt looking at its home.

The evening before, above the noise of the generator, we'd heard the wires of the fence around the yard twanging and vibrating. We grabbed a torch and stepped outside. The beam lit up a wombat grazing on the grass, grass which was long and lush because it was fenced off from the stock. The creature became aware of us and lifted its head to sniff the air, then, unconcerned, continued to graze.

*

The wombat visits us nightly, crashing through the wire fence like a bulldozer, although never breaking a strand. Squat and bear-like in shape with stiff brown fur, wombats are browsing animals and feed on herbage and grasses. We're surprised to see a pair of tiny eyes blinking up into the torchlight between the creature's back legs. We shine the torch closer, and gasp with delight. There's a mass of small claws poking out and nearly trailing on the ground. Our visitor is a female with young.

The animal becomes so used to my presence that soon I can stand half a metre away without disturbing her, although she rarely allows me in front of her head, preferring to turn her back. I sit down on the cool grass and hug my knees. The night is dark and my world is reduced to the beam of the torch, the creature in front of me and the star-filled sky way above. The only sound is the cropping of the grass as she grazes. A calmness comes over me, born of my utter delight in my closeness to this wild animal. I'm enchanted by our wombat and write a children's story about her.

\*

One night, we drive over the dark paddocks towards the rainforest, veering around cattle resting in groups and trying to ignore dozens of wallabies feeding on the grass. After grabbing the torch and leaving the vehicle, we make our way as quietly as we can into the forest bordering a paddock and shine the light up the trunks of the tall gum trees that tower over us.

'There. Look,' Peter whispers.

Two bright red eyes gaze down at us in the torchlight. It's a possum, hugging the trunk way above our heads. There's a noise nearby on the ground, so Peter brings the beam down to reveal another possum scampering along a fallen limb. The animal stops and gazes at us. These are brush-tailed possums, endearing animals with thick dark fur, cheeky faces and long bushy tails. They watch us for a long moment, and we watch them as they go about their business, climbing up and down the trunks of trees and running along high branches searching for fruit, blossoms and eucalypt leaves. The tiny scratching sounds of their feet moving up the bark of the trees reach me and I shiver with pleasure. I want to slip into a hollow log on the ground and hide and become part of the world in which these wild creatures live. I want to climb the trees with the possums, feel the rough bark under my feet and hands and look down upon these strange, huge creatures that walk on two legs. I want to rub my fur against theirs and join in their language. Whatever it is.

\*

The weather gods are kind to us that summer and give us warm, sunny days with no rain or drizzle for a week at a time. Peter and I are relieved to discover that there's decent weather sometimes on the west coast –

although he still wears long johns and fleecy-lined singlets every day. He *had* grown up in the tropics.

I enjoy sitting among the cattle. The ridge to the north of the house becomes one of my favourite places on sunny days. I hug my knees and pick off a grass stalk and chew it as the animals chew their cud in the humming summer silence. Their eyelids slip closed and their ears flick at flies. Unlike dairy cattle, these beef cattle aren't used to being handled, so I'm thrilled that they become used to my presence. There's a salt lick for the stock in one of the paddocks, but, after a while, the heifers lick salt from my hand, their thick, rough tongues scraping the skin of my palm.

Even without the cattle, the ridge is a pleasant spot on sunny days. The grass is thick and lush, and tree-lined creeks meander along at the bottom of the slopes on both sides of the ridge. The ocean is a king's royal blue cape flung to the far horizon, and to the north there's a vast buttongrass plateau, beyond which lies the Pieman River.

\*

Once I know I'll cope with the isolation, I'm as excited as Peter about our venture. Bringing prosperity back to Top Farm is a task worth doing. With hard work, tenacity and luck, we'll turn the property into a spectacular place of undulating green pastures and healthy stock. We'll build a log cabin and improve the track to town. I'll write articles for Tasmanian newspapers, children's stories and maybe even a book one day.

The strength of purpose I feel in our enterprise isn't centred only on the practical aspects. Top Farm has reached deep into my soul. My life on the isolated property fits my yearning for adventure and my inquisitive nature. I've discovered joys I hadn't known existed in the vegetable garden and at the beach and with the cattle. I love the bush and the native animals and feel at home whenever I wander over the paddocks and in the rainforest.

However, only six months into the partnership, Peter and I see a new side of Bob. With only a moment's warning, he hops into the Land Rover and hares off into Zeehan to buy a spare part or make a phone call that could have waited until the next scheduled trip. What's worse, he often doesn't come back for a couple of days. The Land Rover is our only link with the outside world, and there are times when we run out of supplies before he shows up again.

One afternoon, he's about to jump into the Land Rover and drive into town for a spare part for the fertiliser spreader, which, Peter has already told me, could wait until our trip to Zeehan the following week.

'Bob, can't it wait until Monday?' I ask.

'Joanna, how can we expect the rye grass to grow without fertiliser?' He pronounces my name 'Juanna' because he's irritated. He shakes his head and puckers his eyebrows at my idiotic question. 'We can't, can we?'

Resentment flares in me and I grimace, but give in to the inevitable. 'Wait. I'll write a shopping list.'

Fuming at Bob's self-righteous and condescending attitude, I run inside and grab a pen and a piece of paper. I hand him the shopping list and some money.

'I'll be back just as soon as I can.' He grins at me, jumps into the driver's seat and heads off.

When he returns, he brings his wife and a friend from Germany. We greet them as they climb down from the vehicle, but we're shocked when Bob tells us they're going to stay at the cottage for four days.

*What?*

We're to take the vehicle and spend the time at Bob's and Annalies's house on their farm at Oldina.

I can't believe my ears. The cottage is our home. This has been the agreement all along, that Bob's home is at Oldina, and ours is the Top Farm cottage.

My head bursts with anger as I stare at him. I don't want other people sleeping in my bed, picking my ripe tomatoes, finishing off the leftover shepherd's pie in the fridge.

Peter's anger darkens his face and his lips turn into a thin line. Once again, he's caught in the middle between Bob and me. He'd begun the Top Farm venture with faith in our friend, but he's fast becoming pissed off.

Bob ignores Peter. He turns to me and says in his sweetest voice, determined to get his own way, 'Juanna, you can buy yourself a new dress.'

# 5

# Only a leech

I glare at Bob, my whole body trembling with fury.

'C'mon,' my husband says eventually, taking my arm. 'Let's pack a few things.'

Bob's outrageous behaviour adds to the black marks against him. We make the most of a few days on the north coast, shopping for spare parts for machinery and other things not available in Zeehan. I use the time to finish knitting a dark blue jumper for Peter, and we enjoy the luxury of proper showers and television in the evenings. But my husband frets at our absence from Top Farm. There's work to be done there, and he wants to be doing it.

\*

Hundreds of wallabies graze on our pastures every night. Peter and Bob often go out spotlighting with the rifle to control the animals. I hate the idea of killing these creatures, but I can see the reason. As wallaby control is part of our venture, I tell myself to swallow my feelings and go with them.

'The more grass we grow, the more the wallabies breed,' Peter says as we don jumpers and coats after dinner one evening. He picks up the rifle and a box of bullets. 'It's not as if we're killing off the natural population.'

'I know you're right, but I hate the logic of it.'

'You don't have to come.'

'I'm coming,' I say, slipping my feet into gumboots. 'It's part of what we do here, so I need to come.'

'Okay, but you won't like it.'

I shoot him a withering glance and pull on a beanie.

Bob drives the Land Rover over the paddocks while Peter and I stand up in the back, leaning forward onto the roof of the cab. Everywhere I look, I see the dark shadows of the wallabies lit up by the headlights and by the spotlight held by Peter. There are two species of wallaby on our part of the west coast: the Bennett's wallaby, locally miscalled a 'roo, and the smaller pademelon or red-bellied wallaby.

Bob stops the vehicle. Peter hands me the spotlight, which is linked by a long cord to a battery at our feet. My job is to hold the light while he fires.

'Swing it slowly from side to side,' he says in a whisper. 'When it falls onto an animal within range, hold it steady while I shoot.'

I can't judge the distance at first but soon catch on. The beam spotlights a wallaby as if it's on a stage. Blinded by the glare, the animal stays utterly still, ears cocked forward and paws held in front of its body. I look into the large, liquid brown eyes.

*Whump.*

The bullet thuds into the luckless creature's chest. It turns a somersault and flops onto the grass. I cry out and drop the light, which clatters onto the roof of the cab and falls to the ground, lighting up the grass.

'Hey,' my husband shouts. 'What the –'

Bob turns off the engine and throws open the cab door. He retrieves the light and passes it up to Peter.

'Like to go home, Jo?' he asks, not unkindly.

Back at the house, I throw off my gumboots and coat and plonk into a chair, rubbing the back of my hand angrily over my wet cheeks. So much for my lofty sentiments. No one with a compassionate, animal-loving nature enjoys killing wild animals, but the men are tougher than I am. Someone has to do the dirty work. From now on, I turn a blind eye to the wallaby culling.

\*

The intrepid girl who wants adventure goes AWOL when leeches are in the mix. One evening, I decide to go to bed straight after dinner so I can read while snuggled under the blankets. After switching on the bedside light, I soon become absorbed in my book.

Peter is out wallaby shooting on foot. When he returns to the house, switches off the last light and comes to bed, I yawn. My foot touches something cold and wet and slimy at the end of the bed. I shriek and leap up, tossing blankets and sheets into the air.

Startled, he props himself up on a shoulder. 'What's wrong?'

'There's something in there. Down at the end.'

I fumble for the torch on the floor as Peter throws back the bedclothes. The light reveals a bloated, black, slimy creature waving drunkenly on his ankle.

My husband's body sags and he sighs. 'Relax. It's only a leech. Fetch the matches, will you?'

*Huh, only a leech*, I mimic as I pad on cold floorboards into the kitchen.

I like living close to nature, but not *that* close.

\*

One morning when the rain has turned to misty drizzle, I climb into a coat, tie a scarf around my head and exchange my shoes for gumboots. After sloshing through ankle-deep mud to the shed, I kick-start a small Yamaha motorbike which Peter had won in a raffle in Popondetta before we'd left, and which we'd sent by sea to Tasmania, knowing it would be handy on the property.

I putt-putt towards the double dams, enjoying the exhilaration of travelling fast over the ground with the wind in my face. Steers are milling about the dams, some butting each other pretending to fight, others standing and swishing their tails. I watch them for a while, keeping an eye out for any injured or sick animals. Soon, I ford a small run-off from the lower dam and accelerate up a steep grassy slope that leads onto the plateau on the eastern side of the property. I pass a scarlet robin perched on a tussock of grass and soon reach a group of cows in calf gathered at the rear of the plateau.

A lone pipit flies and dances along in front of the bike as I push through an area of bracken fern that's higher than the handlebars. I approach the fireweed paddock, so-called because of the profusion of yellow and red flowering bushes which had covered it when we'd bought the property and which have since been slashed several times, allowing good grass to grow. Here are the Hereford heifers, all heavy with calf. They lift their heads as I check them.

Refreshed and full of *joie de vivre,* I tootle back towards the shed. I suddenly tense as I feel a tickle on the back of my left knee. A slight, unfamiliar pressure.

A leech?

My heart thuds in my chest as I accelerate up the last slope to the shed, park the bike inside and flick my leg to shake off the gumboot. I peel up my jeans and, sure enough, there's a black, slimy, fat, wet leech three centimetres long waving at me from the back of my knee. Shuddering with disgust, I grab a box of matches from the workbench and light one. I twist around and hold it next to the awful creature. After a long moment, the leech sizzles and drops off. I shudder again and see a trickle of blood flowing from the spot where it'd been attached to my skin.

I realise there are itches in other places on my body, too.

More leeches!

I shudder and shiver all over, visualising the ghastly creatures hanging off my body like decorations on a Christmas tree. Frantic now, I rip off my jeans, peel off my socks, and fling off my coat and jumper. I find another leech clinging to the back of my neck – ugh! – and two more colonising the skin at my waist.

I burn off every one with a match, cursing the creatures. After grabbing my clothes, I slide my bare feet into my gumboots and run into the house, where I strip off my underwear and check myself all over.

\*

Each evening after dinner, we read for an hour or so before going to bed. One evening, cosy in our chairs and absorbed in our books, Peter and I hear the familiar roar of a vehicle coming up the hill.

'Probably only Bob,' my husband mumbles into his coffee.

We've been expecting Bob to return for two days, although he doesn't usually arrive this late in the evening.

Yes, it's Bob, with two friends we're thrilled to see: Alison Sutton and Nick House, an English couple we'd known in Popondetta. They'd left PNG before us and had been travelling around Australia in a black and white Kombi van. Months before, we'd given them our Tasmanian address and invited them to stay.

While everyone talks at once, we lead them up the steel steps and into the house. We learn they'd contacted Bob at Oldina then met him at Granville. They hitched up a rope and the Land Rover towed the Kombi along the track as far as Duck Creek.

'It was getting dark, so we decided to wait until tomorrow to bring the Kombi the rest of the way,' Nick explains as Peter hands him a beer. A shipwright by trade, Nick has a thick beard and a wild head of hair. He looks like a seaman of yore who's just shinned down the mast of a sailing ship after trimming the yards. 'You should've seen the old Kombi going through some of those sand drifts, mate! We didn't need Bob to tow us.'

'Ha,' Bob snorts, stowing cans of beer in the fridge. 'You'd still be at Granville if I hadn't come along.'

They haven't had dinner so Ali helps me prepare a quick supper of sausages and bread and butter. Her dark hair frames a creamy English complexion and hides a quick intelligence and enthusiasm for the outdoors. Like Nick, Ali loves visiting unusual places. She tells me about the eight months they'd spent in Darwin and their travels around the east coast of Australia. Ruefully, I realise they've seen more of my country than I have.

The Kombi is to be Ali's and Nick's bedroom while they stay with us. That night, they sleep in sleeping bags on the living room floor.

Early next morning, Peter puts two lengths of heavy chain onto the back of the Land Rover as well as an old tyre, and the four of us squeeze into the cab and bump down the hill and along the track to Duck Creek.

As we round a stony hillock, we spy the Kombi van ahead. It looks forlorn and lonely, standing on a flat spot in sandy, bracken fern country. The men link the vehicles with the two chains, inserting the tyre between them to absorb shocks and minimise jerking. We move off in convoy and begin the drive back to Top Farm.

For some distance, the track is firm and gravelly so the Kombi drives itself. The water level of George Town Packet Creek is so low that Nick fords it easily with the help of a makeshift bridge of driftwood.

Soon afterwards, there's a long, ascending, sandy section of the track which had held up Peter and me for a couple of hours the week before on our way home from Zeehan. Both vehicles stop at the bottom of the sand drift. We gather armfuls of bracken fern and tea tree and spread the branches up and down the wheel ruts in the soft sand to give the Kombi's tyres some grip.

'I reckon we could give it a go now, Nick,' Peter says. 'Drive fast to get a good run-up.'

They start the engines and Peter moves off in the Land Rover, quickly followed by the Kombi. Ali and I stay behind to push.

At first, we have to run to keep up, but soon the Kombi slows with its engine protesting. The wheels spin, spitting fine sand out the back which stings our legs and fills our shoes. The smooth paintwork of the vehicle is cool under my hands as I strain to help push it up the sandy slope. It's no use. Halfway up, the Kombi labours to a halt.

'Look at that tyre now,' Ali says from the front of the vehicle, and laughs ruefully.

The tyre between the two lengths of chain has changed shape from a circle to an extremely thin oval.

It's an unseasonally warm day and we've long since taken off our jumpers. A seabird calls overhead as we gather more bracken fern and tea tree branches and spread them along the wheel ruts. Once again, the vegetation is churned into the deep, soft sand and the Kombi slows to a halt.

We stand on the sandy slope between the two vehicles. Peter rolls a cigarette. Nick, dejected, stares at the Kombi. Ali leans against the Land Rover and crosses her arms.

'There're two new bunks in the house. You can sleep in them if the Kombi doesn't make it,' I suggest.

I receive shocked looks from all three of my companions.

'The Kombi will get there,' Nick tells me, wide-eyed in mock indignation at such an insult to their vehicle.

'Aren't your parents coming to stay?' Ali puts in. 'They'll need the bunks.'

'Joanna, Ali and Nick want their own flat on Top Farm,' says Peter, laughing, and we all join in.

Although I don't say so, I think it's a good idea for our friends to have a bedroom away from the house. It'll give all of us greater privacy.

For now, we're united in the crazy, quirky task we've set ourselves. I'm enjoying the day hugely, fully absorbed in our adventurous undertaking in this deserted landscape. My surroundings all seem larger than life. The sky is a deeper blue than usual; it's glowing, as if lit from within. The bracken fern bushes are a rich, emerald green. The scuttlings and chirrups of little birds and other creatures in the vegetation are clear and pure in the still air, and the smells of salt and bracken and sand fill my nostrils. The company of Peter and our friends is exhilarating, as gleeful laughter and banter fill the air. I'm contented and energetic and in love with life.

Again, we gather armfuls of vegetation and spread them in the wheel ruts. On the last critical stretch near the top, the Kombi crawls upwards, engine screaming, with Ali and me pushing. It reaches a small plateau at the top of the slope. Peter picks up speed and tows the Kombi so far along the next stretch of track that the Land Rover disappears around a sand bank. The stretched chain gouges a long runnel in the bank.

'Phew!'

Ali and I cheer and hug each other.

Grinning and laughing, we walk up the sandy slope to the vehicles. Three hours have passed since we left the farm. I take off my shoes and empty out the sand.

Soon, all of us are standing around the open side door of the Kombi sipping coffee and eating almond cookies in the shape of quarter moons, which Ali had baked in her mini kitchen. Cupboards and shelves line the internal walls of the Kombi between the windows. I spy a small oven and an even smaller fridge, and there are bright curtains and mugs hanging on hooks.

'The table folds down to become a bed at night,' Ali explains.

The two-wheel drive Kombi drives itself for the next few kilometres. From my seat beside Peter in the Land Rover, I turn around and watch Ali's and Nick's elated faces as their vehicle travels under its own power along a rough track that's known only four-wheel drive vehicles in the past.

We arrive at a small creek crossing. Driftwood makes a rough ford for the Land Rover, but it's one which the Kombi can't negotiate. By gathering extra pieces of timber from the surrounding vegetation, Peter and Nick fashion two parallel lanes of logs. Nick drives the Kombi over the makeshift bridge, and we all cheer when he reaches our side.

The Kombi needs to be towed through several more sand drifts and up the last hill to the farm, so it's late afternoon when we reach home. Peter stops and unhitches the chains. Nick drives over the paddocks to the house yard. Ali wants 'a room with a view', so he parks the Kombi beside the paling fence of the vegetable garden. From here, they will look over undulating paddocks and tree-lined gullies to forests and distant blue mountains. Already, the late afternoon sun is brushing the tops of the trees on the far slope with gold.

'This is super,' she says as she gazes around.

Nick and Ali join us inside for drinks. There's plenty to celebrate. We've hauled our friends' bedroom to the farm at the end of the track, creating a record for a two-wheel drive vehicle along our rough road, and we've enjoyed a fun-filled day. What's more, we've thumbed our noses at the isolation.

As soon as Ali learns two horses graze on our paddocks, she's keen to go riding. Thinking of my hair-raising ride on Big Mick, I groan and my stomach churns, yet I want to go riding, too. Maybe I'll be able to handle Pinto?

'D'you want to ride Big Mick, Ali? He's tough and powerful.' I'm hoping she'll say yes, but feel I should warn her.

She's standing beside the big horse's head, stroking his neck. He doesn't snort and back away from her. I groan to myself and my chest tightens.

'Yes, I'll take Big Mick. We'll have a super ride.'

The next day is dry and sunny with a gentle breeze. Perfect for riding. We catch the horses with bread. Pinto's soft, thick lips nuzzle my palm as he takes the slice I offer (it's Zeehan bread). I breathe in his horsey smell and comb his mane with my fingers. He doesn't back away from me. A good start.

We saddle up, mount and walk the horses along one of the gullies towards the stockyards, getting used to the feel of the saddle. The only sounds are the creaking of leather, the swish of hooves in the long grass and the calls of birds. In front of Pinto's nose, Big Mick's rump and tail swing from side to side in time with the movement of his legs. It's pleasant and soothing, although, inside, I'm full of dread.

To my chagrin, Ali handles Big Mick as though he's a child's pony. The big horse obeys every command she gives. I shove aside my feelings of inadequacy and grow more determined than ever to control Pinto. I try to remember what I've been taught in the past. Keeping my back straight, I relax in the saddle and speak softly to my mount, all the time willing him to please, please treat me kindly. The steady plodding gives me confidence and I begin to enjoy the sensation of riding atop a powerful animal.

We cross the gully and meander along the edge of the rainforest on the northern part of the property. I see a scarlet robin among tall grass, then Ali gasps.

'A snake,' she shouts, pointing towards a scattering of branches lying on the ground.

A black tiger snake as thick as a man's wrist and a metre and a half long slithers into dried grass beyond the branches. We give the spot a wide berth and soon reach Newdegate Creek. After splashing through the shallow water, we climb a slope onto the back paddocks of the property. Ali urges Big Mick into a canter. Pinto follows his lead and I try not to tense, knowing Pinto might sense my fear. I press my thighs into his sides and hold the reins firmly.

So far, so good.

We turn seawards. At the top of the hill, we admire the panorama of the distant white sand dunes and rocky outcrops on the coast, and, closer, our tiny house and the Matchbox Kombi.

Ali kicks her heels into Big Mick. He lengthens into a gallop and they disappear over the crest of the hill. I gulp. Following Big Mick's lead, Pinto takes off.

'Steady, steady,' I urge, trying to keep him in a canter. It's no use. In a mad gallop, we fly over the grass, crest the hill and speed down the other side towards Ali and Big Mick. I pull harder on the reins and press my thighs into Pinto's sides, anger tingeing my fear now. 'Whoa, Pinto. Stop, boy. Stop!'

He slows down but turns a complete circle, then another one, much faster. I pull on the opposite reins, but he goes around and around like a ballerina doing pirouettes. The grass spins beneath me. I feel dizzy and light-headed, but red rage is rising up.

I haul on the reins with all my strength. 'Stop, boy! Stop!'

And this time he does. He throws up his head, snorts and stands still. Utterly still. I'm so surprised, my eyes bulge in their sockets.

Glowing with triumph, I pat his neck and stroke his mane. 'Good boy, Pinto. Good boy.'

I speak to him softly as I walk him around the paddock, twice, just to prove that I can. We make our way back to the house and I dismount.

Ali's face is lit up with pleasure as she pats Big Mick.

'That was super,' my friend says.

I couldn't have put it better myself.

*Above: The Land Rover at the bottom of the hill up to the farm. This muddy, wheel-rutted steep track, the only way to reach the farm, gave us many headaches.*

*Right: The Land Rover on the bridge over Squatters Creek.*

*Below: The cottage when we first arrived on Top Farm (not our vehicle).*

*Above: Carried by hand.*

*Right: Strong stockhorse Big Mick gave me a ride over the paddocks that I'll never forget.*

*Below: A horse called Goldie joined Big Mick and Pinto on our paddocks. Unlike the other two, Goldie ate my bread, but he lacked manners.*

*Above:* We took to Top Farm on the back of the Land Rover a second-hand dressing table and a motorbike Peter had won in a raffle before we left PNG.

*Right:* Land Rover fording George Town Packet Creek.

*Below:* The cattle we purchased on the north coast were trucked to Granville and then walked to Top Farm, but two calves arrived motherless. The youngsters were loaded into a crate on the back of the vehicle and driven along the track. Their distressed bellowing brought their mothers out of the bush, udders swinging.

*Above: The Kombi was not designed for the road to Top Farm.*

*Right: English friends, Ali Sutton and Nick House, stayed with us on Top Farm for a month. Our adventures together included a heart-thumping drama on Four Mile Beach.*

*Below: Ali mounted on Pinto. To my chagrin, Ali rode Big Mick as though he were a child's pony.*

*Left: The four of us camped overnight at Conical Rocks, near the mouth of the Pieman River. We caught crayfish and cooked them on the fire, but the benign weather didn't last.*

*Centre: Big red letters high on the rocks: 'Sock it to me Ranch'. Johnno's shack in the foreground with Peter and me standing in front of it. Unfortunately, Johnno wasn't home that day.*

*Bottom: The hill up to Top Farm.*

*Above: The bridge with a broken wing comes into its own – the creek was too deep to ford.*

*Right: Contented cattle.*

*Below: Peter and Yang building the fireplace.*

*Above: Colin Casey showing off.*

*Right: Our vegetable garden, plus a few flowers.*

*Below: Proud of my cauliflowers.*

*Above: Whisky climbing down the ladder.*

*Right: Whisky and a calf in a stand-off.*

*Below: Market gardeners Elsie and Roly Bigwood lived at Granville Harbour and sold their produce to the shops and pubs in Zeehan.*

*Above: Peter leaning on a giant blackwood he'd just felled.*

*Right: At the sawmill – Bob learning the ropes.*

*Below: Friend and midwife Gill Davidson stayed with us for a week when I was nearly seven months pregnant. I was achingly grateful for her presence when my body threatened to give birth to my baby prematurely.*

*Above:* The army carted Top Farm timber to Granville Harbour to give their men 'difficult driving' training.

*Right:* Because of the remoteness of Top Farm, the Zeehan doctor advised me to leave two months before my baby was due. Nicola was born in Canberra. We returned to Top Farm when she was two months old.

*Below:* Nicola and I sitting on timber recently felled by Peter.

*Above: Mum and Yang at the sawmill.*

*Right: Peter and Nicola.*

*Below: Peter and Nicola having fun at Newdegate Creek in summer.*

*Above:* Our tame young Tasmanian devil.

*Right:* A cosy threesome: Nicola and Whisky on my lap beside the fire.

*Below:* Peter, Nicola and Whisky.

# 6

## Lost in white water

While Nick helps Peter with fencing and cattle work, Ali and I cook meals and paint the bedroom blue. This sexism is fine with me. I don't want to wrestle with four-hundred-kilogram steers in the stockyards in order to put numbered tags on their ears and squirt worm medicine down their throats, or spend hours on the tractor slashing bracken fern or spreading fertiliser.

One day, we set off to explore the Pieman River heads to the north of Top Farm. We'll drive along Four Mile Beach then cross Tikkawoppa Plateau.

Four of us in the cab of the Land Rover is a squash but we don't care. With camping gear, crayfish rings and food packed on the back of the vehicle, we're in a holiday mood as we bounce down the hill and trundle along the Granville track until we reach the turn-off to Four Mile Beach. The track to the beach is a pair of wheel ruts winding through sandy country. Bracken fern fronds brush the sides of the vehicle.

'Look! An echidna!'

The animal is at the edge of the track and quickly curls itself into a spiny ball as the vehicle approaches. Peter turns off the engine and we hop out and peer at the creature, surely one of Australia's most intriguing animals. Its quills are yellow with black points and it's covered with dark brown fur. Even as we watch, the echidna digs itself into the ground, literally vanishing into the sandy soil. Echidnas are common but rarely seen, and Peter and I are as thrilled as our English friends to see one close up.

We speed northwards over the wet sand of the beach and ford the creeks which flow across it, all of us exhilarated by the freedom offered by this wide open space on such a sunny, windless day. We've chosen the weather well. Peter and I have never seen the ocean so calm. Tiny waves splash and play at the water's edge, watched by a cheerful blue sky above.

Little do we know what the weather gods have in store for us.

A small bay at the northern end of the beach is named Ahrberg Bay, after a Swedish immigrant who operated a ferry across the Pieman River for close on forty years, until a road was built which connected the west coast towns with Burnie in the north. Johnny Ahrberg carried government surveyors, miners, bushmen and prospectors across the waterway, and occasionally towed a reluctant horse and its rider over – but never cattle, according to Colin Casey, who used to work as a drover.[2]

Before we reach the Pieman River, we have to cross Tikkawoppa Plateau, a vast area of buttongrass that's swampy in places. We crawl along wheel ruts in the moist black soil, veering around bog holes, and after about four kilometres reach drier country of shrubs and wind-pruned vegetation. We circle a hill then spy the mouth of the Pieman River ahead. We slam the doors of the vehicle behind us and walk to the river bank.

The mouth is a hundred and fifty metres wide, and I stare in fascination at the shooting spray and the angry water. A tangle of ocean water surging upstream meets fresh river water head-on, creating the battle in front of our eyes. The roar of the furious water fills our ears and the salty smell is heavy in the air. I'd read about ships being wrecked on the Pieman River bar in fierce gales, often caused by the roaring forties. These are powerful westerly winds that blow across the Southern Ocean.

Over the years, many sailors sought safe shelter in the river, but not all managed to cross the sand bar at the mouth. In 1867, the schooner *Moyne* was one of the unlucky ones. I also thought of the cattle forced to swim across the river upstream. Often, a few head were swept down to the mouth, and, unless they managed to scramble ashore, were drowned.

The Pieman River was named after a convict escapee from the Sarah Island penal settlement who crossed the river on an improvised raft on his way north in 1822. His name was Thomas Kent and he was known as 'the Pieman'.[3] The image of runaway convicts pushing through our rainforest, tramping along Four Mile Beach and crossing Tikkawoppa plateau fires my imagination. I often try to picture these desperate, starving men making their way up and down mountains and through tangled forest in the hope of finding a lonely fisherman or a prospector's shack. I wonder how the Indigenous inhabitants reacted to these men with pale skins and strange garments.

We head upriver along a gravel track. The spot where Johnny Ahrberg had operated his ferry is a little way upstream near a hamlet of holiday shacks. We're immediately struck by the neatness of this settlement. Even though corrugated iron is, inevitably, the favourite building material, the walls and roofs of every dwelling glow with fresh paint. The shacks stand in a park-like area of mown lawns and scattered trees. Marigolds bloom in garden beds and children play among the buildings.

We hop down from the cab of the vehicle.

A man emerges from a dwelling set back among a stand of trees. He's tall and the skin of his face is thick, like leather, with a colour that resembles the tannin in west coast creeks. 'G'day, there,' he calls out as he strolls over to us. 'Name's George. Come from far away, have you?'

'Top Farm,' Peter says, shaking his hand and introducing us. 'Moved onto the place some time ago.'

This seems to establish us as more than mere tourists in George's eyes. He invites us into his shack for a beer. We learn that he runs a service station in Burnie with his son, but his heart is on the west coast where he'd grown up.

'I come down here as often as I can to fish and yarn and relax. You ought to come to our next New Year's Eve party. We throw whopping parties.'

Peter and I look at each other.

'Thanks, we'd love to,' I say, meaning it, yet knowing it's not feasible. The unpredictable weather and the hazardous route rule out partygoing.

'Say g'day to Johnno when you reach his shack at Conical Rocks,' George says when we leave. 'Can't miss it. Sock It To Me Ranch it's called. Johnno's a cray fisherman.'

\*

We wave goodbye to George and follow the track back to the mouth of the river, then meander south along the coastline, searching for a camp site. No sandy beaches here. The ocean meets a shore dominated by enormous pink boulders and rocks many metres high. Inland from these rocks and boulders, the track crosses a soggy buttongrass plain where we quickly become bogged. Nick is driving and curses into his beard. We jump down from the cab and cross to dry ground. I leave behind a gumboot bogged in the mud, and groan. After pulling off my sock, I squelch back to retrieve it, the cold, black mud oozing between my toes.

We always carry a spade, a wallaby jack and half a dozen long planks on the back of the Land Rover. Ali and I gather sticks and stones to go in the wheel ruts, while Peter and Nick dig out some of the mud in front of each tyre. They jack up the wheels and slide a plank in front of them. Peter hops into the driver's seat and tries to drive out but the muddy wheels spin helplessly on the slippery planks, shooting them out the back like arrows.

Soon afterwards, Nick comes across a long pole in the rocky landscape, a lucky find. He positions one end of the pole under the back of the Land Rover and rests the other on his shoulder. When Peter engages the clutch, Nick pushes the pole upwards and helps heave the vehicle out of its muddy hole.

Wow! What a sight! He's Atlas, the demigod in Greek mythology condemned to support the sky on his shoulders. I congratulate Nick and ask for a photograph. He pretends to heave the vehicle out again while I click away. We giggle with the silliness of it all and scramble back into the Land Rover.

After rounding a bend in the track, we come across a weird sight: a rough dwelling with makeshift walls and a corrugated-iron roof, and at each corner of the structure there's a worn-out wheel with a flat tyre.

Behind the shack huge pillars of granite rise to the height of four-storey buildings. Giant letters are scrawled across them in scarlet paint. 'Sock It To Me Ranch' the letters scream at us.

'Johnno the cray fisherman's shack,' I say.

'He must have towed the dray to this spot, then built the shack on top of it,' Peter muses.

Johnno isn't home. We're disappointed to miss him as he's evidently a west coast character.

Soon, we find the ideal spot for a camp site, an area of firm sand sheltered from the ocean by pink granite rocks several storeys high. After pitching the tents on the lee side of the rocks, we gather firewood for a campfire before deciding to try our hand at catching crayfish.

Crayrings are rings of steel about a metre in diameter covered with coarse mesh rope. We climb up and over the rocks to the seaward side, where the boulders and rocks form a rough horseshoe shape enclosing an inlet. High above the water, we find niches on which to perch and gaze down at the surging ocean. As each wave recedes, the level of the water drops many metres, exposing huge tendrils of bull kelp which stretch outwards and invite the next waves in.

The power of the ocean awes me. Exhilaration races through my veins as I breathe in the salty air. I wave to Peter and Ali away to my left on another rock, and to Nick further around the inlet, all of us beaming at each other. The crashing of the waves on the rocks is so loud that we can't hear one another, even if we shout.

Holding onto the end of a long rope attached to one of the rings, Nick throws the ring into the water. Peter does the same with the other ring. It isn't long before a crayfish and half a dozen large crabs are caught in the mesh of one of the rings. Their nippers and legs thrash wildly as Nick hauls it up. Peter's ring has caught another crayfish. As dusk falls, we make our way back to camp. We cook our catch in a pot over the fire and throw potatoes into the coals to cook. The air is chilly but a roaring fire and the thrill of camping in a wild place keep us warm until we snuggle into our sleeping bags.

Awake early next morning, I'm immediately aware of a different sound.

Lying beside me, Peter puts my thought into words. 'The sea's changed.'

My neck is tense with alarm as we scramble up the rocks. Freezing water shooting up from the inlet drenches us as soon as we reach the top. The gentle swell of the day before has been absorbed by an angry ocean that pounds the rocks with cannonballs and shatters water into thousands of droplets.

Peter and I stare at each other with wide eyes. What about the beach?

\*

We trundle south over Tikkawoppa Plateau, peering ahead. A hazy, swirling mist hangs over Four Mile Beach. An ominous sign. There's silence in the cab of the vehicle. Peter drives down the track onto the end of the beach and we meet a screaming wind head-on, which fills my ears, even inside the vehicle. I try to make out what's happening. Through the haze, I glimpse mighty waves shooting high up the beach, their tops torn off by the fury of the gale.

'Jesus.'

'Shit.'

Pushing the door open against the powerful wind, we climb down from the vehicle. I have to lean into the wind to stay upright. Now I know the meaning of the west coast saying, 'If the wind stops, everyone falls over.' But none of us is laughing. Peter and I exchange grim looks. Vehicles have been lost on Four Mile Beach. Will ours be next?

Trying to gain protection from the wind, we crouch in the lee of the Land Rover to eat our lunch of leftover crayfish, tomatoes, bread and butter. Even in the partial shelter of the vehicle, flying particles of sand sting our faces and crunch between our teeth. We have to shout to hear each other over the wind.

My stomach muscles tighten as I stand up and peer over the bonnet of the vehicle at the flying mist and the heaving grey sea ahead. If the Land Rover gets swamped on the beach, it will set back our Top Farm venture.

Beside me, Peter's mouth is set in a tight line but he lifts his shoulders. 'We have to go. The weather could worsen and we'd be stuck here for days.'

Nick drives. Wind batters the vehicle as we move along the wild beach. Our English friend zigzags: driving on wet sand as the water recedes, then veering inland to avoid the crashing waves.

A gigantic wave leaps up the beach in front of us.

'Christ,' Nick mutters.

We plunge into the wave and are lost in white water like a plane in cloud. In front of my face, frothing seawater cascades down the windscreen. I grip the front edge of the seat beside my legs with tight fingers. Beside me, Ali groans. The ocean swirls all around us, seeping through the bottoms of the doors as Nick drives on, slowly.

'Phew,' someone says. 'That was close.'

Spoken too soon. The engine dies. The Land Rover stops. The ocean is swirling around us.

'Water's got into the distributor, Nick,' Peter yells as he grabs a rag and jumps out.

Nick follows and they throw up the bonnet. In the cab, Ali and I look at each other, the shock on her white face reflecting my own. I hear water surging around the wheels, and imagine it drawing sand away from each tyre. I look through the driver's open door, and gasp. The wild, grey ocean is swelling with another huge wave. A hot, tight feeling squeezes my chest.

A lifetime later, Nick jumps in and turns the key. The engine farts once, then starts. Peter slams the bonnet and leaps into the cab as Nick engages the clutch and we lurch off, leaving the new wave in our wake.

We approach Newdegate Creek which, the day before, had been a shallow trickle. Now, deep water surges up and down the sandy channel with every wave.

'Seawater's gouged it out,' Peter yells as he jumps out and searches for a place to cross.

The vehicle nosedives as Nick drives over a sand cliff into the channel, but soon we are across. We bowl along, zigzagging in a mad race to beat the incoming tide. We manage to ford Squatter's Creek.

Soon afterwards, Nick's quick eyes see a hillock of dry sand ahead, just in time to veer around it; if we'd ploughed into that, the vehicle would've been stuck like Winnie the Pooh in the door of Rabbit's house.

At last, we draw closer to the far end of the beach, where a sandy hill covered with bracken fern beckons us through the spray and mist. We still have to cross George Town Packet Creek, which flows into the sea just below the hill. By now, we aren't surprised to see that the width of the creek has trebled since the day before. It's six metres wide and goodness only knows how deep. Waves surge along the channel, banking up so much water that the overflow floods the surrounding sand. Eddies and whirlpools rise and fall with each wave.

Peter jumps out to find a place to cross. My eyes follow his hurrying figure as he runs up and down the eroded sandy cliffs of the creek.

The vehicle is sinking into the saturated sand, I can feel it.

'Christ,' Nick shouts as he throws the gears into reverse.

The vehicle refuses to respond. Twice we stall, sinking deeper. I suck in my breath. On the next attempt, he succeeds and reverses out with a lurch.

Peter signals for us to cross at the spot where he's standing. We wait for the angry water to recede, then Nick guns the engine. We plunge over a sand cliff into the channel. The water is so deep we create bow waves on each side of the vehicle. A new wave surges up the channel, deepening the water and swirling into the bow waves, but the Land Rover keeps going.

We roar up the sandy track leading away from the beach. I let out my breath and slump onto the back of the seat, grinning at Ali beside me.

Nick stops at the top of the slope. He pokes his head out of the window and grins at Peter, trudging up behind us. 'Sorry I left you behind to get your feet wet, mate.'

My husband squelches up to the vehicle, smiling with relief. 'Where's the beer?'

Ten minutes later, we stop beside the track and dig out four cans of beer from the esky. Sitting cross-legged on a patch of moss, animated by feelings of sheer relief, we talk non-stop as we gaze at the glorious sight of the Land Rover on dry ground. Beer isn't my favourite drink, but I'm so relieved the vehicle is safe that I drink a whole can of it. When it's time to go, I lurch to my feet and, tipsy but happy, climb into the vehicle.

\*

Sitting alone at my desk the next morning and writing up my diary, pondering the hazardous trip the day before, I realise that I thrive on the dramatic and exciting incidents in our lives. I remember my terror during the wild ride on Big Mick; my fear when riding Pinto then my joy when I mastered him; the suspense as we carried two steers on the back of the Land Rover – all these incidents prompt emotions of fear, suspense and excitement, followed by utter relief. My zest for life is fully aroused, with every cell in my body on alert and every sense heightened. Just as I'd felt on that pipe on Nowra Hill and on the swaying foot-bridge in Papua, I feel fully alive when experiencing that heady mix of exhilaration, fear and suspense.

# 7

## 'We must call him Whisky'

Ali and I cling like monkeys to the mudguards and roll bar of the tractor and try to keep hold of overflowing laundry baskets. The day is warm and sunny and Nick is chauffeuring us to Newdegate Creek, where we'll wash the clothes; with little rain in the previous week, the water in the house tank has to be kept for drinking, cooking and showers.

Nick has improved the route from the pasture down to the creek by flattening dogwood trees and widening and levelling the track with the blade on the tractor. The scent of crushed dogwood hangs in the air. Our vegetable plants and flowers have already received a drink after Nick brought back a forty-four-gallon drum of water from the creek.

Ali and I sit on rocks with our bare feet in the water and work up soapy lathers on jeans, underwear and sheets, then wade into the middle of the creek and anchor the garments with rocks to be rinsed. They stream out in the current like flags and little fish swim in and out of the folds. Our chatter mingles with the sound of water splashing over rocks upstream and I feel like a village woman doing her washing in the timeless, primitive way.

That frivolous notion doesn't last long. Thank goodness, it rains soon afterwards and we can wash at home. Besides, the beauty of Newdegate Creek deserves more than dirty clothes.

*

With Ali and Nick, we drive to Trial Harbour, a village of fishing shacks similar to the one at Granville Harbour. Peter and I have never been into this seaside hamlet, even though we pass the turn-off on every trip to and from Zeehan. Like Granville, Trial had been used as a 'port' in the past, but the inlet is little more than a break in the rocky coastline, and there's no wharf or jetty.

The four of us stroll around the settlement, huddling into our coats against the chilly wind. Shacks built of fibro, scrap timber and corrugated iron line the makeshift streets. Remains of early shops are here and there, built partly of bricks and timber scavenged from the convict ruins on Sarah Island in Macquarie Harbour.

Trial Harbour was named after a seven-ton cutter called the *Trial* that was owned and manned by four Baltic sailors in the 1880s. For six years, the cutter made scores of trips to the 'port', anchoring in the inlet to deliver supplies to Heemskirk miners and to take out their tin, but her end came when she foundered after five days of battering by mountainous seas.[4]

The history of the west coast continues to surprise me and ignite my interest and imagination. The salt-laden wind blows into my face as I gaze at the heaving sea in the inlet. I picture those sailors unloading cargo from the cutter to a dinghy which takes the goods to shore, and for the hundredth time marvel at the resilience and toughness of the early Europeans in this wild place.

Ali gasps. 'Look at that.' She's pointing to a massive chimney that dwarfs the shack to which it's attached.

Consisting of dozens of pieces of corrugated iron patched together, the chimney covers more ground than the dwelling itself. The pieces of corrugated iron are coloured red and beige and rusty brown and resemble a pyramid pointing to the sky.

'An untidy patchwork quilt,' I say.

Stepping carefully and thumping our feet on the ground in case of snakes, we make our way through the bush on the slopes above Trial, and are surprised to come across a stamping mill rusting in a patch of heath. Three metres high, with upright metal posts and attachments so rusty they are rotting before our eyes, the machine had been used for crushing ore. Its presence reminds us that the west coast had been swarming with miners eighty years before.

At the beginning of her stay, Ali had said of the isolation, 'As long as I've got a good book to read, I'll be fine.'

Like me, she's a bookworm, and it's this that helps keep things harmonious in the house, for Ali and I are together most of the time. When Peter and Nick are outside working and we've finished the household jobs, we pick up our books and become lost in our own worlds. I'm reading *Watership Down* by Richard Adams, an unlikely tale about rabbits that captivates me from the first page.

On other occasions, my English friend retires to the Kombi to sew or read, while I take a cup of tea or coffee into the bedroom and sit down at my desk to write letters and bring my diary up to date.

Even though I've grown to enjoy solitude on the farm, I like having Ali's company. We often tramp over the property and into the rainforest. We talk and laugh and exchange stories of our adventures in other parts of the world, our childhoods and everything in between, such as what to do when falling out with an old schoolfriend, and the best way to cut toenails. With scissors or clippers?

Occasionally, there are minor disagreements in the kitchen, such as on the morning we cook a sponge cake and disagree about when to take the hot cake out of the tin, but they are rare.

My one big emotional reaction to Ali's visit is the inadequacy I feel in comparison to her. She is so much more accomplished than I am at so many things. She's a good horsewoman, a whizz at cryptic crosswords and a much better cook than me. At her suggestion, we make savoury pies for picnic lunches. Her recipe for a boiled fruit cake is one I've used ever since.

In my self-absorption, I don't stop to think what Ali's feelings might be, or reassure myself about my own abilities – I feel I don't have any. My feelings of self-doubt and inferiority aren't any of Ali's doing. She simply takes everything in her stride – or seems to, whereas I struggle. Inside, I am often cringing and shrinking back, as though I'm not good enough.

These thoughts sometimes spiral down into a general feeling of profound inadequacy, a feeling that everyone else is 'better' than me, a vulnerability that has been with me ever since I can remember. Whether this deep-seated lack of confidence is a result of having been to half a dozen schools in my primary years, at each one of which I was the new girl, standing alone in the playground; or whether it comes from my situation as an only child without a sibling with whom to fight; or even from the example of my parents' relationship with each other, I do not know.

Yang was loving and affectionate and cracked silly jokes, but he was also authoritarian: the breadwinner, the boss and the head of the household in every way. Mum was cuddly and loving, a sensitive, artistic person who enjoyed painting in oils. She was a whiz at needlework, especially smocking, and as a seamstress she could turn a length of fabric into a chair cover or a stylish dress. But my darling mother lacked inner confidence; she was totally submissive to her husband. 'Barbie even asks Will when to breathe,' my dear Auntie Margie used to say of her sister.

Perhaps it's inevitable that I, too, am unsure of myself with others.

Yet as a deeply loved child with parents who wanted only the best for me, I developed, contrarily, a strong sense of self.

Perhaps this is one reason why the natural world appeals to me. Nature doesn't judge. When I'm in the bush, I'm not comparing myself to other people. There's no possibility of others judging me, or, more tellingly, me judging myself as wanting.

Nature also teaches me, by example, to be myself. A eucalypt blossom sheds its little cap without any thought of whether or not it should.

When I'm in the natural world, I feel whole inside.

\*

On their way to Tasmania, our friends had called in to see my parents in Canberra, and had picked up Peter's record player and two big speakers, as well as all our records. On their last night on Top Farm, we turn the living room into a disco and dance until midnight to music by Buddy Holly, Neil Diamond and the Everly Brothers. It was a fitting end to a special time. Ali's and Nick's visit strengthened my growing love for the farm at the end of the track.

*

My parents come to stay for the first Christmas we spend on Top Farm. They sleep on the bunk beds and hide their anxiety about our isolation and the financial riskiness of our venture. I know they are worried because they love me to bits and want to see Peter and me settled and secure. 'Darling, do you really like it out here?' they ask. I reassure them I am happy – as I've been doing all my life.

Their concern is understandable. With no telephone or two-way radio, we are on our own in an emergency. Not until much later when I have children of my own do I realise the worry they must have felt.

Christmas Day in 1974 is the unforgettable day when Cyclone Tracy screams through Darwin, the capital of the Northern Territory. The eye of this tropical weather depression passes over the city between midnight and seven o'clock in the morning. Torrential rain falls and the gale-force winds are officially recorded at 217 kilometres an hour – before the Bureau of Meteorology's anemometer is destroyed. Sixty-five people are killed and most houses and buildings are destroyed. All public services – communications, power, water and sewerage – are severed.

In the little cottage on Top Farm on that Christmas morning, my parents and Peter and I exchange gifts and huddle around the transistor radio listening to news of the devastation in Darwin. The reception in our radio is poor, so the broadcast fades in and out of our hearing, a frustration felt most keenly by Yang, who'd spent two of the war years stationed in the northern capital with the RAAF, where he was a photographic reconnaissance pilot.

Bob arrives soon after Christmas and he and my father get along famously, perhaps as only two former combatants can. Fuelled by a bottle of whisky, they go hammer and tongs in vigorous discussions about the war, politics, military strategies, the best vehicle for Top Farm and a dozen other topics, conversations which both of them enjoy hugely.

*

If there is one thing that turns a house into a home, it's a fireplace.

While Mum and I paint the living room walls, Yang and Peter design a brick fireplace and chimney for the cottage. Most of the bricks are old fire bricks from the disused Zeehan smelters. The others have been given to us by Frank Mihalovich, the caravan park owner in Zeehan. Like many of the people we meet on the west coast, Frank's interests are unusual. The caravan park is his day job. The real love of this tall man with a triangular face and a beard is mining crocoite at various sites on the west coast. Crocoite is a valuable red crystal with the proper name of lead chromate.

Peter brings the bricks out to Top Farm on the back of the Land Rover. He and Yang mix ingredients to make the mortar and begin laying the bricks. Yang helps until he and Mum leave a week later. They incorporate an ash-drop below floor level, pipes for hot water at the rear of the fireplace and a horizontal iron bar at the side that swings out over the fire to hold a pot of vegetables or stew or soup. A small door on the outside of the chimney allows us to remove the ash outside, rather than carry it through the house to the door. (Some months later, I am achingly grateful for the ash-drop when I do the most careless thing I've ever done in my life.)

In a climate that is frequently chilly, rainy and miserable, the fireplace becomes the focal point of the house. There are evenings when Peter loads up the fire with so many huge logs that we have to retreat to the back of the room. 'Enough heat to melt the south pole,' Yang quips on a later visit to Top Farm. The welcome warmth, the noise of crackling, sliding timber and the fragrance of the wood fire create such a feeling of well-being and camaraderie that our worries seem a long way away.

Yet at other times I'm mesmerised by the leaping, twirling orange flames, and wish I could see the future in the flashes of blue that appear then vanish like the mists of a dream.

*

One day, Peter goes to town and comes home with a climbing rose in a pot and a ball of black and white fluff in a box. I peer into the box. Two big eyes stare up at me and I grin with pleasure.

Mum looks over my shoulder and smiles. 'He's black and white. We must call him Whisky,' she says.[5]

The kitten settles into farm life. We laugh at his antics in the living room, scold him when he sharpens his claws on the furniture, and feel sick when he eats blowflies, purring as he crunches each mouthful. Ugh. His fur is soft beneath my hand as I stroke him on my lap in the evenings with my feet stretched towards the fire.

During the day, Whisky often prowls through the paddocks. He's unafraid of those giants, the cattle and horses. He steps right up to their hoofs and sniffs, leaping away like quicksilver when the hoof moves. When Peter goes out shooting at night on foot, Whisky quickly learns it's a good lark to go with him and gorge on newly killed wallaby meat.

In fine weather, one of his favourite resting places is on top of the gatepost at the bottom of the yard. Like a king, the cat holds court with the cattle. The heifers amble up and gather around him, intrigued by this tiny creature sitting quietly with its tail curled around its body. Whenever one of the heifers pushes her nose too close, Whisky's paw shoots out and cuffs her. The heifer leaps backwards with hoofs crashing, startling all the others behind her. They bound away, kicking their heels high in the air. Whisky gazes after them, regally disdainful of such playful behaviour.

Our adolescent cat has no dignity when he stalks the currawongs, however. One day, a currawong is perched on a corner post. With his four legs hunched up like a spider's, Whisky creeps up the diagonal post support towards the bird. Eyes rivetted on his 'prey', apparently unaware that he's in full view of the bird, he moves closer and closer. When the currawong finally flies off, Whisky utters a weird, huffing cry of anger.

One day, three currawongs notice Whisky chewing a bone on the grass. They stalk up to him and scare him away and again he utters that huffing noise of anger as he retreats, leaving the bone to the birds.

I love having a pet. Often alone, I enjoy his company, whether he's rubbing himself against my leg in the kitchen or lying curled up on an easy chair. I laugh when he teases the cattle and grin when he's intimidated by the currawongs. I feed him titbits and enjoy the sound of his deep purring as he lies on my lap by the fire.

\*

I plant the climbing rose beside a fencepost in the yard. With a spade, I turn over the soil and enrich it with fertiliser, then dig a hole and place the little plant carefully in the hole. Tending the rose becomes one of my daily joys. I erect a little fence of chicken wire around it as protection. I have visions that my rose, the symbol of civilised gardens, will grow and climb and bloom its way all around the fence and, together with other flowers we are cultivating, turn Top Farm into a botanic garden at the end of the track.

Alas, I am only dreaming. The climbing rose is chilled by cold south-west winds and chewed by cattle who lower their heads over the top of the fence. Later, when we acquire half a dozen hens, the poor rose is pecked by the free-ranging birds who poke their beaks through the wire. My rose is tenacious, however, and struggles on.

\*

One night, unearthly screeches yank us out of sleep.

'What on earth?'

'Grab the torch.'

Cracking shins and stubbing toes, we fumble our way to the kitchen and feel for a torch on the shelf. We shine the beam through the window and see two Tasmanian devils fighting over the remains of a crayfish we'd eaten the night before. The snarling animals tumble and wrestle and tear at each other with lightning speed, scattering the contents of the rubbish bin all over the ground. They break apart to crunch up more crayfish shells then abruptly return to the fight, a fight so ferocious you'd think it would be to the death.

My bare feet grow cold on the floorboards but I don't care as I watch, fascinated. Weighing six to seven kilograms, devils have a large head and massive, powerful jaws. They feed on carrion, wallabies, possums, birds, snakes, lizards, insects and even rabbits and rats. The animals are black with white markings but these two look scruffy with sparse tufts of fur on their backs. They alternately eat and fight, screeching all the time and ignoring the torchlight. The unearthly screeches don't cease until they lollop off into the night.

This encounter is so thrilling I can't go back to sleep. Excitement fills my head and my body is alert as I lie in bed replaying the scene in my mind. We'd watched wild animals behaving as they do in the wild. A rare treat.

Not long afterwards, I grab the opportunity to spend a day in the field with zoologist and devil researcher Dr Eric Guiler of the University of Tasmania, who is studying devils on the Bottom Farm.

Eric Guiler is a stocky, tanned Irishman who laughs easily and calls all devils 'George'. I accompany him and his assistant, Mr Sward, in their Land Rover as they check traps they'd set the day before along the edges of paddocks, on farm tracks and on game trails. The traps are drop-door wire cage traps about a metre long by half a metre high and wide.

We drive over a paddock to a trap set beside a dead cow. Sure enough, there's a devil caught in it, eyeing us with suspicion as we climb out of the vehicle. The cow has been half-eaten.

'No doubt the cow'll be finished off tonight,' Dr Guiler says.

Stock deaths from natural causes augment the food available to devils from wallabies shot by Don and Jim in their game control operations.

Thrilled to be involved, I watch and take photographs for a newspaper article. I cling to the dashboard as we bounce over the paddocks and find three more devils caught in traps. The animals are weighed, measured and sexed, and the females are examined for young in the pouch. Each is tattooed if caught for the first time. Devils are powerful creatures with strong, lethal jaws, so how do the men tattoo a devil's ear?

'Carefully,' says Dr Guiler with a grin. 'We take a hessian bag with one corner cut out, and manoeuvre George until an ear pokes through the hole.'

Working together, he and Mr Sward transfer the animal from the trap into the bag, which bulges and jerks about as the devil tries to escape. In the time it takes me to snap my fingers, they have manoeuvred the creature so that an ear pokes through the hole.

Dr Guiler explains he's chosen Granville for his study because it's an isolated spot. 'There aren't many people around so there's minimal human interference in the devils' activities. The farm is accessible by four-wheel drive vehicle, so it's easy to carry traps around the property.'

The object of his study is to observe the population structure and the numbers of devils over a period of years, assess the breeding success and the lifespan, and obtain knowledge of the movement pattern of the animals on the west coast to see whether or not they are territorial in habit. He tells me there aren't as many devils on the west coast as there are in other parts of Tasmania. Because of geographical features – mountains, rainforests, the Pieman River, Macquarie Harbour – the west coast animals are isolated from those in the rest of the state, which underwent a population explosion in the 1960s.

Around four o'clock, the zoologist and Mr Sward free the last devil from its trap, examine it, and let it go. The animal lollops over the paddock into a belt of bush along a creek.

A currawong calls overhead and a breeze ruffles my hair as we lean on the bonnet of the vehicle.

'How long have you been studying devils here, Dr Guiler?'

'Around ten years.'

Two of the devils caught that day already had tattoos on their ears, meaning they'd been caught before. I ask him how many animals he's caught and recaught.

'I'll send you the figures when I get back to Hobart, Jo.'

Later, I learn that quite a few 'Georges' have been caught many times. Dr Guiler has trapped a total of 282 different animals 946 times.[6]

The next day, Dr Guiler comes to Top Farm to see first-hand the conditions for devils in our part of the world. We drive all over the property then talk over morning tea. Until I went to Tasmania, I'd confused devils with the Tasmanian tiger, or thylacine, a carnivorous marsupial with stripes across its rump that had thrived in the Tasmanian forests until the European colonists arrived with their sheep and their firearms. The last known thylacine had died in Hobart Zoo in 1936. Was the species extinct, or wasn't it?

We ask Dr Guiler his opinion but he's non-committal. I show him some dried animal faeces which Bob found in the forest one day and now insists on keeping in an old Vegemite jar on the bookshelf (behind the books). Bob believes the faeces come from a thylacine because they're too big to be from a devil.

With scientific care, Dr Guiler turns the Vegemite jar around in his hands and peers at its contents. 'This is from a devil. See the bits of bone?' he says, shaking his head. 'A tiger would eat the soft parts of the kill – heart, lungs, kidneys, a bit of flesh from the thigh. They leave the bones to the devils.'

He explains the manner in which a thylacine kills its prey, which leads to great excitement several months later.

Regarding the faeces, our partner, when he returns to the farm, doesn't want to take Dr Guiler's word for it that the specimen belongs to a devil. 'I've known other so-called experts who've been wrong,' he tells me, his eyebrows raised arrogantly.

'He's a scientist,' I say, astonished. 'He's been studying devils for years.'

Bob shrugs away my words.

*

As we trundle homewards along the track on a drizzly afternoon following a trip to Zeehan, with a second-hand chest of drawers and a small table tied on the back of the vehicle at odd angles, Peter and I arrive at Sandy Beach, a beach which always seems to attract more than its fair share of bull kelp. Heaps of giant brown spaghetti cover the sand, and the Land Rover slips and slithers through until we reach a patch of grass beside the shack at the back of the beach.

In the middle of the inlet, a dinghy is rising and falling with the slow ocean swell. A man is sitting in the dinghy next to a black metal box, which, Peter tells me, is an air compressor.

'Brian must be underwater,' he says, as he turns off the engine.

As he speaks, a marine monster emerges from the water and climbs up onto rocks. It's Brian, dressed in a black wetsuit and flippers. He gives us a wave. Soon both men are coming ashore in the dinghy. They cut the outboard motor and ask us into the shack for a cup of tea.

While Brian peels off his wetsuit, I see that the alcove in the hut is crammed with fishing paraphernalia. I step through a doorway into the main room. Socks hang on string across the front of the fireplace and paperback books and boxes of matches sit on the mantelpiece. A frayed carpet covers the floor and a wood stove stands against a wall beside a neat pile of sticks and logs. Wind buffets the outside of the shack, rattling a loose board, but it's cosy inside with the smell of salt and woodsmoke hanging in the air.

We learn that Brian and Dave, his companion, live in Devonport on Tasmania's north coast. Like other professional fishermen and abalone divers, they come down to the west coast when the weather's good and the sea calm.

I sit on a couch that sags in the middle and sip tea from a pink china cup that's chipped on the rim. I blink and stare at it, remembering the delicate blue and white handle from a china cup unearthed when Peter and I were turning over the soil for a vegetable garden at Top Farm. A flush of pleasure surges through me at this confirmation of my idea, but Brian interrupts my thoughts.

'Bob's in his fifties, isn't he?' He's standing by the fire sipping tea from another chipped pink cup. He's thoughtful for a moment. 'Beats me why he wants to get mixed up in a farm after all those years in PNG. He should retire and put his feet up.' He pushes wet hair out of his eyes. 'He's a rum 'un, all right.'

'Some people can't retire, Brian,' Dave puts in. 'I reckon you'll be one of them.'

'Nah.' Brian grins and shakes his head.

'We'd better get going,' Peter says, standing up.

'Like a fresh crayfish?' our host asks, swallowing the rest of his tea. 'I'm going back in. I'll get a couple for you.'

Half an hour later, we climb into the vehicle and continue on our way with two newly caught crayfish wrapped in newspaper between us on the seat.

At home, I make a seafood sauce using tomato sauce, Tabasco sauce, Worcestershire sauce and tinned cream. I serve the crayfish on a bed of shredded lettuce, with sauce added. The dish is tasty and tender and utterly luscious, but it's thanks to Brian's fresh crayfish, not to my culinary skills.

\*

Cattle prices begin to fall, and soon they're falling as fast as our savings. At the beginning of the venture, a fair amount of our money had gone into the partnership as our contribution towards the cost of the land, equipment such as the Fergie tractor, the generator, the fridge and stove, and many smaller items. Since then, we've purchased cattle and regularly spent money on food and fuel. Peter and I listen to the news on the radio about the decreasing value of cattle with concern, but live thriftily, determined to hang on until the market improves; we don't know it, but this is the beginning of a slump from which the cattle industry will take years to recover.

One morning, I awake feeling weary and worried. After breakfast, I do the washing up then make a cup of coffee, strong and sweet and flavoured with cardamom seeds, a habit I'd begun in PNG after Peter and I visited a friend on his cardamom plantation.

I carry the hot mug into the living room. Damp clothes hang from a clothes horse in front of the fire, which I'd lit earlier, and I fuss over them, removing the dry garments and spreading out the others. The slither and crackle of burning wood is the only sound as, dejected, I sink down into a cosy chair.

Restless, holding the coffee, I get to my feet and drift back into the kitchen and stare out of the window. Green pasture, grazing cattle, distant blue mountains. An egret in the yard.

I draw in a breath and let it out slowly. With no money coming in and little left to live on, we face an uncertain future.

# 8

# A fish on the end of a line

> Curse the wind
> Curse the weather
> Curse the west coast altogether[7]

Peter and I discover that winter on the west coast means rain and more rain and still more miserable rain. I wouldn't mind the rain except for the bitter cold. I wouldn't even mind the rain and the cold except for the freezing wind which howls out of the south-west, rattling the windows and finding its way into the house through the bathroom bullet holes, down the chimney and through ill-fitting skirting boards. When I'm outside chopping kindling or tending to the vegetable garden, I have to lean into the wind to keep my balance. I've never experienced wind so strong, constant and cold. It whistles down my neck, creeps up my sleeves and penetrates six layers of clothing.

The cold, lashing rain makes a lot of mud. There's mud at the front steps of the house, mud at the paddock gates and mud all around the shed where the tractor and Land Rover re-churn it regularly. Everyone and everything gets bogged. The cattle, the vehicles and us. I grow sick of the mud outside and sick of the mud tramped into the house. Even though all of us take off our gumboots in the alcove, the shoes into which we slip our feet carry globules of mud into the kitchen and the living room, so there's always mud left on the floor, adding to the housework.

Worst of all, the rain turns the hill up to the farm into a two-hundred-metre-long mudslide. Made of mudstone which turns to grease in wet weather, steep, and criss-crossed with deep wheel ruts, the hill terrifies me. Going down in the Land Rover resembles being on a slippery dip for vehicles.

Our worst trip to town takes place after two hundred millimetres of rain have fallen in two weeks. Our supplies are low, so we have to go. We climb into the Land Rover and set off at seven o'clock in the morning and drive out of the farm gates to the top of the hill.

The rain has turned the hill into a gigantic muddy slope. We slide and skid down at precarious angles and I cling to the metal dashboard with fingers that turn white from fear. Peter drives the vehicle down with a confidence and skill I never learn to share. In several places, there are vicious corners of wheel ruts and gullies to negotiate, and at other times we are slithering downhill sideways, sideswiping dogwoods growing at the edges of the track. Somehow, we don't tip over. Finally, we arrive at the bottom of the hill, pointing in the right direction. I breathe out and loosen my fingers.

Peter drives over a large granite boulder and then through a little creek that flows across the track, missing by centimetres a one-metre-diameter eucalypt log lying beside the track just beyond the creek. He has to keep up the revs to get through the creek as it has a soft bed, but as soon as we are through the wheels grip the firm surface of the track, and he has to make a quick manoeuvre to avoid the old gum.

The wet sand on the first section of the track is solid beneath the wheels so we make good progress until we crest a sandy rise covered with bracken fern and see the track ahead disappear into a new lake twenty metres long. Tips of bracken fern and tea tree poke above the surface of the water like periscopes.

Peter turns off the engine. Two black ducks take off from the lake, the flapping of their wings loud in the cold, still air.

He finds a long stick and wades into the water and leans out as far as his gumboots will allow to test the depth. 'It's okay,' he says at last. 'Not too deep. The track here is solid, so we won't get bogged.'

We cruise through the lake. For the second time, I admire bow waves from the vehicle.

No bridge is visible at Squatter's Creek. Instead, a torrent of floodwater surges across the track. The creek rushes along with a life of its own, carrying branches, leaves and tangled debris, much of which becomes caught up on vegetation growing on the banks, creating eddies and more tangles.

I frown as we stand at the edge of the water. 'We've got to come back along here later,' I say. 'The creek might be even wider and deeper this afternoon. Maybe we should go back home.'

Yet we need butter and flour, meat and milk, soap and torch batteries. Besides, there'll be longed-for letters from friends lying in our postbox.

'Looks as though the rain's stopped,' my optimistic husband says, studying the sky. 'The water will've gone down by this afternoon.' He wades into the flooded creek and pushes his way across the invisible bridge, feeling for the decking with his gumboots. 'The decking hasn't been washed away,' he calls out. 'We can drive across.'

I grab the dashboard and hold my breath as we drive through the floodwaters over an invisible bridge across an unknown depth of cold, dark water. I don't breathe again until we climb out the other side.

Four kilometres further on, we drive over the lip of the gully down to George Town Packet Creek, and groan. This is the bridge that resembles the broken wing of a bird, where the creek flows beneath the decking on one side then emerges in the centre through gaps in the planks. But today the water is much higher than usual and we cannot see the decking of the bridge at all. Instead, the flooded creek swirls through debris piled up on top of it.

The creek was named after a cutter shipwrecked off the coast way back in 1874. According to a report in Launceston's *Cornwall Chronicle* on 13 January 1875, mariner Charles Mullins and his mate, James McClutchery, left Launceston on 3 December 1874 in the *George Town Packet*, a small cutter rigged vessel of twelve tons, 'for the purpose of procuring mutton birds and eggs'. All went well until 19 December, when the wind, blowing hard from the north-west, drove the vessel towards the coast. 'On the evening of 20 December, finding all hope of saving the cutter gone, I determined to run her ashore in order to save our lives,' Mullins said. 'The vessel at the time was leaking badly, had lost all her bulwarks and stanchions, and would have soon foundered, as her deck had started. I headed her for a sandy spot and after passing through about a mile of broken water, during which time we had great difficulty in holding on to the vessel, she struck, and in a few minutes broke up into fragments.'

The sails of the *George Town Packet* were washed ashore along with a precious bundle which Mr Mullins had thrown overboard and which included matches and dry blankets. With the blankets, the two shipwrecked sailors made 'a rude tent'.

At first, the men headed south towards Macquarie Harbour, but the going was tough. Disheartened, they turned around. They crossed the Pieman and Arthur Rivers by raft, using some of their blankets to fasten pieces of wood together, and reached inhabited areas in the north on 2 January.

The story had absorbed me from the first time I'd read it. Here were two sailors who were shipwrecked somewhere along our own Four Mile Beach, which made them seem very close. Not only that. They managed to survive. I knew there'd been countless mariners lost on this treacherous coast of whom nothing was ever heard again.

\*

Peter and I look at each other and back at the racing floodwaters. The debris piled up on the bridge consists of a tree trunk and a tangle of branches and twigs and leaves, with the torrent swirling through it. The only way for the vehicle to cross the creek is by fording it.

I climb down from the cab in my gumboots. With one foot after the other feeling for the decking of the lopsided bridge beneath my feet, I make my way across, clambering over the debris, to watch from the other side. With the vehicle in low ratio four-wheel drive, Peter drives into the rushing water. The current must have created a deep channel in the middle of the waterway because the vehicle abruptly nosedives. Through the windscreen, Peter's face registers shock. As he moves slowly forward, water comes up to the headlights and laps the bonnet. As the Land Rover begins to level out, the inevitable happens. The engine dies.

Peter opens his door and climbs onto the mudguard. He opens the bonnet and dries out the distributor cap, spark plugs and coil then climbs back in to the driver's seat and turns the key. The engine refuses to start. He does this several times but there's no response.

I sigh and slide my hands deeper into the pockets of my coat.

For a moment, nothing happens, then the vehicle jumps forward, once, twice and again. Jerkily it emerges from the creek, shedding water like a submarine.

Peter drives a few metres then stops and hops out. 'That's called grinding it out with the starter motor,' he says with a grin. He had turned the ignition key with the gear engaged and the clutch pedal out.

'Surely that can't be good for the engine?' I say.

I receive a glare.

'Do you want to go to Zeehan today, or don't you?'

I look away, suitably chastened, as he bends over the engine and dries out the important bits with a rag. We don't speak. The sound of the water rushing along the flooded creek is loud in my ears.

The vehicle starts with a fart. I open the passenger door to climb in but icy water flows out, straight into my gumboots. Hell's bells! That icy water penetrates my socks and freezes my feet. I gasp and stare downwards as my feet turn to ice. They *ache* with the iciness. I glance up at Peter, who begins to laugh. He laughs so much he drops his cigarette onto the watery floor where it goes out with a hiss.

I start laughing, too, somewhat hysterically when I realise I have no dry socks.

We trundle on along the track, lurching and spinning our way through a long mudhole until the wheels grip again on the far side and we drive out of it. The worst parts of the track are behind us, but the rain has created many new washouts which have to be negotiated with care. A huge mass of bull kelp is strewn across the beach in front of Brian Jago's shack. We slip and slither through tendrils as thick as a man's arm and see several tree trunks that have been tossed high up the beach by the storm.

A pair of sea eagles hovers in the sky and a family of four quail on the track ahead scuttle into coarse grass beside the road as we approach. We drive through Granville and over the buttongrass country. Close to Zeehan, where the track leads us through thick forests of myrtles, blackwoods and tree ferns, there are dozens of muddy patches that threaten to bog the vehicle, but Peter thwarts them all. At half past eleven, we drive along the main street of Zeehan and park outside the post office.

Zeehan is a town in which grand buildings rub shoulders with humble miners' cottages. The post office is an ornate, two-storey stone structure with arched windows. Beside it stands the courthouse and Gaiety Theatre, both in the same style. These buildings give the central town area a gracious charm left over from the mining boom in the late 1800s and early 1900s, when the town's population reached nine thousand.

A bitter wind greets my emergence from the Land Rover. I pull my coat tightly around my body as I hurry to our postbox. When the little black door swings back and I see a pile of letters in the darkness, excitement races through me.

I meet Peter in the quaintly named 'Dinning [sic] Room' of the pub over the road after he's collected the newspapers, which the newsagent keeps for us. Beige linoleum covers the floor and the furniture is utilitarian, but the pub is warm and we know the food is good. We settle ourselves at a table. Peter sips a beer and I ignore my lemon squash as I eagerly scan the handwritten letters from my parents and from friends in PNG and Canberra. We order counter lunches of spiced meat loaf and apple pie but it isn't until I begin eating that I realise how hungry I am. For a short time, I stop poring over the precious letters and eat, leaving the pages scattered over the table.

Reluctantly leaving the pub's warmth, we drive to the supermarket at the other end of town and stock up on meat, fruit and groceries, then pick up a forty-four-gallon drum of petrol at the garage. Because I'm pregnant, I can no longer do up the zippers on my jeans and slacks, so I buy some elasticised material in the drapery shop to sew into the front of each pair. Afterwards, I head to the medical centre for an appointment with the doctor.

'Where are you planning to have the baby?' Dr Arnold asks me.

'Queenstown Hospital. It's the closest.' Queenstown is about half an hour's drive south of Zeehan.

'No, no, no.' He leans forward over his desk and peers at me. 'You're too far away out on Top Farm. Is there somewhere you can go when you're seven months' pregnant?'

'Seven months?' I stare at him in shock. 'Really?'

The doctor spreads his hands. 'It's not safe to stay any longer in such an isolated spot.'

I sink back in my chair as I take in the news. I am four months' pregnant. That means I'll be leaving the farm in three months' time, in October.

\*

We head out of town around two o'clock in the afternoon accompanied by a cold drizzle. The sky is dark with promise of more to come but that turns out to be the least of our worries. Just past Granville, the Land Rover becomes bogged in a long, deep mudhole. Thick, black and sticky, the mudhole resembles a block of chocolate in hot weather. The vehicle sinks to its axles and our spirits sink with it. Peter turns off the engine and jumps out without saying a word. His mouth is set in a straight line and I know he's furious with himself for getting bogged.

Beside the mudhole, a green and red corrugated-iron toilet shed lies on its side, and there's an old iron bedstead nearby. These abandoned pieces of civilisation emphasise the bleak isolation of the spot.

The top half of each wheel of the Land Rover is all that's visible above the mud. We begin collecting stones and driftwood from the rocky coastline. At each wheel, Peter crouches down in the mud and uses the rocks and driftwood to build up a base for the wallaby jack. As he jacks up each wheel, I push more stones under the front of the wheel and, eventually, the end of a plank. Our hands are black with mud but at last there's a plank sticking out from the front of each tyre.

We still haven't talked. The only sound is the harsh 'kurrak kurrak' of plovers wheeling in flight above a sandy hillock not far away.

Peter climbs into the driver's seat and tries to drive the vehicle out but only manages to spin the wheels and shoot the planks out backwards. When he jumps out of the cab, his cheek muscles are tight. Again he jacks up the wheels and pushes more stones and driftwood underneath them. We scrape the mud off the planks before wedging them in again.

The wheels spin and spit mud but begin to move forward until the right rear wheel shoots its plank out backwards and sinks deeper than ever into the mud. I groan. We've been stuck for nearly three hours. I suggest we walk back to Granville and ask Viv Coleman to tow us out with his four-wheel drive vehicle.

Peter glares at me.

Standing in the cool air with my fingers crossed that we'll get the vehicle out soon, I sigh with frustration and wish for the hundredth time that our track was a decent one. Weariness and despondency threaten to overwhelm me, yet I am utterly committed to Top Farm. We simply have to cope with troubles like this as best we can.

On the third try, the Land Rover heaves itself out of the bog as though it's as eager as we are to go home. I feel like cheering and dancing. For me at that moment, happiness is getting out of a bog. Peter and I pile into the cab and speed off, chatting happily, even though we're both aware there's now no hope of reaching home before dark.

Winter's early dusk soon reduces our world to the track lit up by the headlights. When they shine onto the black water of George Town Packet Creek, we both sigh wearily, our cheerfulness evaporating. Not much rain has fallen during the day, so we'd hoped the level of the creek might have gone down, but it hasn't.

Peter uses plastic bags from the groceries to cover the electrical parts of the engine. Once again, I scramble over the debris-strewn bridge to watch from the other side. In the darkness, I slip and knock my shin on a branch and wince with pain, but it's worth the weird sight of the vehicle's headlights travelling under water.

Further on, Peter studies Squatter's Creek in the light of the headlights and wades across the invisible bridge as he had in the morning. Water swirls around his gumboots.

'Several planks have been washed away but there are enough left. It's safe to cross.'

With the wheels aligned above the main bridge bearers beneath – and my fingers gripping the dashboard in front of my face – we bump and splash halfway across the bridge, then the vehicle lurches sideways and drops. I cry out and tighten my fingers, expecting to fall into icy water.

'The wheels have concertinaed some loose planks,' Peter tells me. 'That's all.'

We reach the other side of the creek without mishap and drive up the side of the gully.

Cold, tired and hungry, we long for home. We reach the base of the hill up to Top Farm at ten o'clock that evening. Peter gets a good run-up at the bottom of the slope, but the poor, protesting vehicle quickly becomes bogged in half-metre-deep wheel ruts.

'We'll have to walk up the hill,' I say, stating the obvious, as he turns off the engine.

'Yep. And tow the Land Rover up in the morning.'

I close my eyes, pressing my eyelids together, refusing to think about the morning.

Hampered by darkness and by gumboots heavy with mud, we tramp around the vehicle, transferring the food from the vehicle's tray into the cab, not wanting devils or tiger cats to eat our hard-won supplies.

Clutching steak and other food, letters and a *National Geographic* magazine that arrived in the mail, we start to climb. A little moonlight filtering through clouds gives shape to trees and the track as we plod upwards, often slipping and cursing, our caked gumboots adding extra weight to each step. At last, we reach the paddocks. Puffing, I stop and draw in a deep breath, my weariness now overlaid with a feeling of relief and gratefulness that we're nearly home.

On grass now, we climb more sure-footedly to the top of the hill, from which we can see dim outlines of the shed and the house welcoming us two hundred metres ahead.

As I fumble in the dark kitchen, a slow, labouring pulse beat breaks the night silence, becoming faster and more rhythmic as the generator gets into its stride and slowly illuminates the light bulb hanging from the ceiling. I light the fire I'd set early that morning. It crackles and grows into a fierce blaze. I throw some potatoes into the fire and grill steak and tomatoes on our gas stove.

After eating this on our laps, we toast bread bought in town over the fire and eat it dripping with butter and jam. No steak, potatoes or toast has ever tasted so good. I snuggle into my cosy chair with my feet stretched towards the fire. Whisky jumps onto my lap. His fur is soft beneath my hands. Satiated, sleepy and warm at last, I lean back in my chair as contentment flows through me.

\*

I rise next morning to a bleak and drizzly day. My heart is beating faster than usual. Dread fills my stomach and there's an unfamiliar tightness in my neck muscles.

My gumboots become caked with mud as I slip and slide down the hill to the Land Rover at the bottom. Peter drives the tractor from the shed to the top of the hill. He walks down and attaches one end of a long chain to the chassis of the vehicle. I climb into the driver's seat and slam the door.

'Start the engine and keep it running,' my husband tells me through the window. 'If your wheels start to spin, let up the accelerator.'

'Right,' I say, determined not to be timid, although I'm so fearful my hands are wet with sweat.

'I know the track's slippery, but don't worry.' He gives me a tight smile. 'You won't tip over.'

'No?'

'No.'

I grimace as I wipe my hands down my jeans. Clutching the steering wheel, I watch Peter climb up the slope to the tractor and engage the gears. The chain between the two vehicles tightens and lifts, flicking mud from the links. The Land Rover creaks and begins to move upwards.

Soon it's leaning at an awful angle and sliding sideways. The wheels fall into a rut and it nearly tips over. I gasp and grip the steering wheel more tightly, concentrating on watching the tractor wheels way above me, my shoulders rigid and my heart thrashing in my chest. Slowly, inexorably, the vehicle and I are pulled upwards, coming back to the vertical as a different wheel rut guides us out of a ditch.

The drizzle turns to rain. In front of me, the wipers swish from side to side and keep the windscreen clear. I can no longer hear the tractor through the pouring rain. I can't see it either. All I can see through the windscreen is the chain leading upwards and the clay hillside, crisscrossed with deep, muddy wheel ruts. All I can hear is the roar of the Land Rover engine and the regular beat of the wipers.

Concentrating intently with all of my senses on full alert, I hug the steering wheel as though it's a life line. Hauled up by the chain and guided by the zigzagging wheel ruts, the vehicle travels diagonally for a few metres. A bump and a lurch, and the right-hand wheels fall into a ditch. I crash against the door and cry out. We're leaning so far over, that, when I glance through the driver's window, I see tiny pebbles among the mashed wet clay half a metre from my face.

Sliding uncontrollably at the end of the chain, the Land Rover and I fall into a gaping ditch on the other side of the muddy hill. I'm a fish on the end of a line, unable to control my fate. Terror surges through me, even though my brain tells me nothing serious can happen. Can it?

My neck muscles are stiff. I try not to panic as we're hauled up sideways. I'm now hugging the steering wheel with the whole of my body. The rain grows heavier and streams down the criss-crossing wheel ruts up ahead, creating little waterfalls. The roar of the engine fills the cab.

The rain eases and I see that the big wheels on the tractor are spinning. I let the clutch out a little so the Land Rover's gears become engaged, but our wheels start to spin, whirring mud. However, the momentary loss of drag behind the tractor has stopped *its* wheels spinning, so on we go, lurching up out of one set of wheel ruts only to drop all four wheels into another set.

Anger is beginning to tinge my nervousness now, anger at this rotten hill and the rotten west coast weather. The tractor wheels spin again and, this time when I engage the clutch, the Land Rover drives itself for a short distance, to my astonishment. A feeling of power surges up in me, but an instant later I realise the chain has disappeared under the left-hand side of the vehicle. *I must not run over the chain.* I stop, balancing the clutch and accelerator so we don't slide backwards, and wait for the tractor to take up the slack again.

In his seat on the tractor, Peter turns round and bellows down the slope, his face black and his free hand gesticulating wildly. I've got no idea what he's saying. Sudden rage fills me. I poke my head out of the window and scream back, furious with him, the hill, the vehicle, the farm and the whole of the west coast with its lousy weather and rotten roads.

The tractor takes up the slack. The chain jerks up and flicks mud into the air. I glance out of the passenger window and gasp. We are sliding sideways towards a wheel rut that resembles a bomb crater, but the chain hauls us up and beyond it. I sigh with relief.

The Land Rover and I are hauled up the rest of the hill without any more wild rides. We reach the grass at the top. I stop the vehicle and breathe out.

Peter unhooks the chain. My fear and anger have evaporated and we exchange grins. I drive the vehicle the rest of the way home under its own power, grinning to myself and filled with a fierce elation. We have beaten that wretched hill.

# 9

# No mail

By now, cattle prices have fallen so much that the cattle are no longer worth the cost of transporting them to sale yards. The problem has arisen from the huge size of the Australian cattle herd and the loss of some export markets. Deeply worried, I walk to Newdegate Creek one morning and sit on the bank. I feel with my fingertips the texture of bark on a tree, see a kingfisher dip down onto the surface of the water for a drink, and marvel at the beauty of a fern frond unfurling. My neck is tense as I stare into the water and try to see the future. What do the coming years hold for us?

A breeze touches my cheek and I hear a plop as a fish jumps. The peace and beauty seep into me.

\*

Peter, Bob and I sit in front of the fire, the bleak outlook enveloping us all in a gloomy mood. To make Top Farm viable, we need another source of income, and fast. We're aware of the high value of blackwood in the timber market, and we know our rainforest is full of blackwood trees. Do they have commercial value? If so, we could install a small sawmill on the property and see out the downturn in cattle.

Golden to dark brown in colour, usually strong-grained but occasionally yielding to 'fiddleback', which gives a three-dimensional effect, blackwood is a beautiful timber. We research the market on the north coast and learn that it's in great demand both in Tasmania and on the mainland, principally as a furniture timber. The manager of a sawmill on the north-west coast says he will purchase as much as we can supply, both as flitches and in planks of smaller dimensions. Excitement speeds through me and Peter's face lights up with optimism.

'Means we can stay on the farm,' he says.

Bob finds a company which manufactures a portable sawmill that would be ideal when set up at the edge of our rainforest. We also need to purchase a bulldozer to snig logs, a four-wheel drive tractor and a trailer to haul the timber to Granville, and a lot of smaller equipment such as a jib which will work off the smaller Fergie tractor. The jib will be used to load the bundles of timber on to the trailer.

It's drizzling outside on the day the three of us pore over columns of figures on pieces of paper spread over the dining table. The figures show estimates of income and expenditure, all in thousands of dollars, but they look realistic and the bank has agreed to give us a loan. Nevertheless, the proposal to snig and mill timber in rainforest where the ground turns to mud in the slightest drizzle, and to transport the sawn planks along a hazardous track, is a highly audacious one. Are we crazy to even consider such an idea? Financially, we'll be taking a huge risk. If the venture fails, we'll be forced to sell the farm to pay off the mortgage. Peter and I will have to leave the place which is our home as well as our business. We'll have no money, no job and nowhere to live.

Yet if we don't embark on the timber venture, that scenario is, without a doubt, our future.

The logs in the fireplace crackle and pop as we talk. We're all optimistic that problems can be overcome. We're determined to make a go of Top Farm.

'What d'you think?' Bob asks as he sips his syrupy coffee, flavoured with several teaspoons of sweetened condensed milk.

We're eating fresh bread I've just taken out of the oven. The hot steamy aroma rises into my nostrils as I bite into a slice on which butter has melted into golden pools. After many attempts, I can now bake a decent loaf. Pleasure spurts deep inside me as I watch Peter and Bob tucking into their slices.

My husband is enthusiastic. He loves Top Farm and wants to stay. And me? I can't wait for the timber venture to begin. I'm keen to make a go of Top Farm. I believe in its potential to produce cattle or timber or both. Besides, this place is home now and I feel settled. I enjoy our daily life and the simple but real pleasures it offers. With a baby on the way, the last thing I want to do is move.

Peter looks at me and I nod. He grins and turns to Bob. 'Let's do it. It's a goer, as long as we can get the timber to Granville. The track'll be the problem.'

'It's winter,' I put in, trying to be realistic even while my heart thumps with eagerness to begin. 'There'll be more rain.'

Peter rubs his chin. 'We can't wait for spring.'

Bob finishes his bread and leans back in his chair. He slaps the table, his eyes lighting up and his face shining with enthusiasm. 'Full steam ahead.'

\*

There's a great deal of work to be done before we install the sawmill. The men spend many days working on the worst parts of the track. This pleases me no end. Timber or no timber, I am all for making our trips to town easier. Maybe one day I'll be able to drive myself to Zeehan, meet other women and join a writing group, or, when the baby is older, a playgroup?

Although I love the solitude that Top Farm offers, I also, at times, long for company, or at least to connect with other people. That's why letters from Mum and Yang and friends are so important – and why I'm distraught one day when Bob returns to the farm without the mail or the postbox key.

'Jo, I left the key at Oldina,' he states as he dumps two bags of groceries onto the kitchen bench.

*What?*

In the alcove of our little house, I stare at him as my jaw drops. The world around me tilts. I see Bob standing in the house, I hear his and

Peter's voices, I smell the fragrance of a cake I've just popped in the oven, but raw bitterness fills my mouth. For a long moment, I'm in another place, a place of deep, dark, desperate disappointment. Letters from friends and Mum and Yang replace conversations that aren't possible in my remote life. It's been a while since the mail was collected. I know there'll be many envelopes thick with letters waiting for Peter and me in our postbox, but I can't get my hands on them.

Peter sees my disappointment and hugs my shoulders. 'The mail will still be there when we go to town next time.'

I nod. It's all I can manage.

\*

Forgetting the key is an innocent oversight on Bob's part and I don't try to explain why I'm distraught. Letters mean so much because they're my only way of feeling close to friends and my parents, the next best thing to being with them. A letter is a connection between two people, offering support and empathy. There's mutual interest in each other's lives. Reading the handwriting of a dear friend gives me a warm glow inside.

Every letter is different in size, thickness, texture and even smell. Excitement sparks deep inside me when I recognise, instantly, the handwriting on an envelope, handwriting that's as unique as a friend's face. As I slit open the envelope, the sound of the tearing paper fills me with joyful anticipation. I draw out the folded pages and begin to read, and immediately I'm absorbed in renewing a bond with a friend in a genuine and deeply personal way.

Most of the time, my satisfying daily life fills me up, but the desire to regularly connect with others close to me is still there.

\*

In preparation for carting timber to Granville, Peter and Bob dig new drains along the track, rebuild Squatter's Creek bridge and lay a causeway of logs in the big mudhole in which Peter and I had been bogged some weeks before. The bridge over George Town Packet Creek, the one with a broken wing, won't need repairing as the tractor will ford the creek.

On fine days, I walk from the farm to the spot where they're working. One day, there's an echidna among the bushes on the top of a sand bank at my eye level. The creature is shuffling around gathering ants and termites with its long sticky tongue. Interested, I watch for a long time as it continues to feed, heedless of my presence.

Back on the farm, Peter and Bob clear a flat area of land near the double dams as a site for the sawmill. We've purchased a bulldozer. Peter fells trees in the forest which Bob drags to the mill site with the 'dozer. The logs are embedded in the earth on one side. They will provide a firm base on which the mill logs will be rolled up to the saws. The men construct a large shed with a corrugated-iron roof, but no walls, over the area where the sawmill will be erected. Finally, they dam a nearby creek to provide water for the engine and to wash dirt and debris off the logs before they're sawn.

The new sawmill arrives at the farm in pieces. Some are on the back of the Land Rover, others on the trailer behind our newly bought, second-hand, four-wheel drive tractor. On a cold day punctuated by violent rain squalls, Peter and Bob begin to assemble the mill with the help of the sawmill's designer who's flown over from Melbourne for a couple of days.

To my surprise, I'm interested in what's going on. Not only because the sawmill represents our future, but also because it's an intriguing thing and sparks my curiosity. The basic components are small and simple: a steel framework, a diesel engine and two circular saw blades, one horizontal and one vertical, which travel with the engine along the top of the log being sawn. The framework can be adjusted to raise or lower the saws for larger or smaller logs. The clank of metal and the shouts of the men compete with the noise of the freezing wind that flings rain under the roof of the mill as they work.

\*

We hire a professional tree feller to fell enough blackwood trees in the forest to give us a stockpile to start milling. Thereafter, Peter will do the felling, a prospect which frightens me. Bringing down huge trees is a dangerous job, but if he's daunted, he doesn't show it.

I study Eric Farrow's boyish round face and smooth complexion as we sit around the dining table late one afternoon over cups of tea, just after he's arrived in his vehicle. A big man in his late twenties, Eric is a woodchop champion who can cut through a thirty-five-centimetre log in thirty seconds and a bushman who wields a heavy chainsaw all day long. His shoulder muscles push out his old black and yellow football jumper like pads on an American gridiron suit.

'Black tea. Two sugars, please,' he says in answer to my question. He has a gently modulated voice and a natural graciousness that appears at odds with his line of work. He will stay with Peter and me in the house, sleeping on a bunk in the spare room, and he'll begin work early next morning.

Conversation turns to the dangers of felling trees as an occupation.

'Trees have nerves, like all growing things,' Eric says, indicating a sensibility not often credited to men who work in the bush. 'They fall in different ways according to their quirks.'

'Quirks?' Whisky jumps onto my lap and purrs as he curls himself into a ball beneath my hand. 'What sort of quirks?'

'Each tree has to be assessed differently,' our visitor says, leaning back and holding his cup in both hands.

A pink spot appears on each of his cheeks. I suspect he's ill at ease talking about himself.

'I look up at a tree, see what natural slant it has, if there's much wind, whether there are any unaligned or broken branches which might get hung up on a neighbouring tree.' He pauses and shrugs, making light of the perils of the job.

Whisky jumps down from my lap and wanders past Eric, who puts out a hand and strokes him.

'I also look at the trees nearby and decide if there's any possibility of whiplash,' he goes on. 'If the tree is going to strike a nearby tree on its way down, you don't want any limbs left hanging, so perhaps you'd fell that tree at the same time.'

'How?'

'Cut one tree partly through, then cut the other. As it falls, it takes the first one with it.'

'Just how dangerous is this job, Eric?' Bob asks.

'Peter will do the felling after you,' I put in with a grimace.

'Jo, it's usually over-confidence that kills,' he says reassuringly. 'Most of the fellers killed by trees are experienced blokes who've been doing it for years.'

\*

Next morning, Peter, Bob and I watch Eric at work in the forest. Holding the chainsaw with both hands, he looks up to the top of the chosen tree to assess it before deciding where he wants it to fall. He starts the chainsaw by holding it with his left hand and dropping it the length of his arm while pulling the starting cord with his right. The scream of the chainsaw fills the air as he cuts a wedge out of one side of the tree. After stepping behind the tree, he cuts through from that side.

We watch from a spot many metres away. I tilt my head back and fasten my eyes on the foliage high in the forest canopy. For a heartbeat, nothing happens, then the top of the tree begins to move and gains speed, and the mighty blackwood smashes its way down through neighbouring trees, branches and vegetation, and crashes onto the forest floor. The very earth vibrates, and I feel the vibration through the soles of my boots. Afterwards, there's an eerie silence, a silence which, I later realise, is the forest's tribute to the giant that has fallen.

Eric fells over thirty trees on his first day, dropping them inwards to the centres of large circles to make snigging easier. Not until then do I realise the extent of the damage we're inflicting on the rainforest. I had visualised trees being cut down and lying on the forest floor in among the flourishing lower plants and vines, but my imagination hasn't prepared me for the utter destruction I witness. Saplings and tree ferns are smashed, and vines, wildflowers and fungi vanish beneath tangles of leafy debris and the trunks and branches of the mighty trees that have been brought down. And all the while the scent of crushed leaves and moist soil hangs in the air.

I am aghast, shocked and saddened at the devastation created in the forest. At first, I can't reconcile the necessity of generating an income with the destruction of such natural beauty. When we'd first come to Top Farm, I'd been captivated by the natural world all around me and the adventurousness of living in such an isolated and spectacular place.

I still feel that, but over the next few days my naivety gives way to a realistic, practical view. Even more devastating than the destruction of the rainforest is our dire financial situation. Peter and I are eking out the last of our savings. It's as if daily life is built on a foundation of sand, and the sand in the hourglass will run out sooner rather than later. It's profoundly unsettling, and robs me of peace of mind and well-being. Walking into the supermarket in Zeehan with only enough money in my purse for the most basic of items; not going to town at all because we can't afford to buy anything; being unable to pay a personal account – all these things leave me with a hollowness inside, a growing desperation about the future.

'You'll more than pay your way with that sort of blackwood,' Eric tells us that first night as we yarn around the fire.

Immediately alert, I sit up straight and have to stop myself jumping up and hugging him.

'It's the best I've seen on the west coast and there's not much like it in the rest of Tassie.'

Peter and I exchange grins, elated to hear such an opinion from one who knows. Although I regret what we are doing to the forest, I turn away. Top Farm is home. Milling blackwood will bring in money and enable us to stay.

\*

During his time on the farm, Eric fells enough trees to keep the mill going for about ten days. To help with the work of snigging and milling, we employ a young Zeehan man whose name is William but who's nicknamed Tank because he's built like one; he lives with Bob in the caravan. The bulldozer drags the logs one by one to the sawmill, where they're washed and milled. Gusts of freezing wind drive rain under the roof of the mill and onto the backs of the novice sawmillers. Thirty centimetres of rain fall that month, double the monthly average. Soon, the earthen floor of the mill is ankle deep in mud, while outside the mud is even deeper. It cakes boots and hampers every movement.

The saturated soil plays havoc with the 'dozer. Twice the machine slips a track on a steep, muddy slope in the bush. The tracks are made of heavy metal links, and each time the men spend hours getting the track back on, a frustrating job in deep mud.

And all the time the rain falls and the mud deepens.

'When the going gets tough, the tough get going,' Bob says ruefully one evening after he, Peter, Tank and I have shared a meal and are sitting around the fire. He sighs. 'By gees, it couldn't be much tougher.'

Whisky jumps onto his lap and claws his thighs. He winces and shoos the cat off, who strolls over to me with his tail in the air.

'There's spring around the corner,' I put in, determined to be optimistic as I welcome Whisky onto my lap.

Peter grimaces. 'That corner's still a long way away.'

Despite the difficulties, the men turn out dozens of sawn planks which will be sold to the north coast timber merchant.

\*

If bringing down the trees causes a lot of damage to the rainforest, putting a bulldozer in to drag them out is akin to letting a gigantic mixmaster loose on the undergrowth. The bulldozer and the log slithering and bouncing along behind it crush countless ferns, vines and shrubs, and gouge ugly wounds in the fecund topsoil. I often walk in the forest and watch what's going on. Native laurels, tree ferns and fungi, and leatherwood, blackwood and myrtle saplings are smashed and crushed and left in ragged rows along the edges of the new tracks.

However, my sensibilities fade away at the welcome prospect of generating an income.

\*

Peter starts felling blackwood trees and I start worrying. A few of the trees are as thick through as a man's height, but even the smaller ones can be killers. Whenever he heads out in the Land Rover with the chainsaw on the back, I grow tense with concern. I hear the scream of the chainsaw as it cuts through the trunk of a tree way off in the rainforest. I stop what I'm doing, stand utterly still and wait. The noise of the chainsaw ceases and there's silence for several seconds, until the sound of the tree crashing to the ground reaches me.

It's then that I hold my breath until I hear the chainsaw screaming again, which tells me he survived that one.

'Be careful,' I say at breakfast most mornings.

'I'm always careful. I'm a cautious man by nature.'

'What if a branch gets hung up as the tree falls, then crashes to the ground when you least expect it?'

'I won't be standing in the way.' He leans over and touches my arm. 'Don't worry, sweetheart.'

I stand at the kitchen window and try to reassure myself. Peter had learned a great deal from Eric Farrow. Eric had commented that only complacent fellers are killed. Peter is cautious by nature.

None of this helps.

# 10

# Paddling upstream

The worst problems in our timber venture occur on the track to Granville. One drizzly morning, Peter, wearing wet weather gear of yellow waterproof trousers and a yellow hooded raincoat, sets off on the four-wheel drive tractor to tow the first load of timber to Granville Harbour. The plan is to stockpile the sawn timber at Granville, where the north coast timber merchant will collect it and transport it to Burnie.

However, after fording George Town Packet Creek, Peter cannot get the tractor and trailer up the steep incline just beyond the creek. A long run-up to gain speed and momentum is impossible because, immediately beyond the ford, the track turns sharply to the right as it climbs steeply out of the gully. He curses and repeatedly backs the tractor down into the creek and tries again at different angles to reach the top of the slope, but the angle is too sharp. Furious and frustrated, he walks back to the farm.

He and Bob decide the only thing to do is to rebuild the bridge so it can take the weight of the four-wheel drive tractor and the timber. If the tractor uses the bridge rather than the ford to cross the creek, the corner will be wider, enabling the tractor to get a greater run-up to climb the slope.

We're all worried, however. Time is running out. We need to have the first stockpile of timber stacked at Granville by the following Friday, when the timber merchant is due to pick it up. That's seven days away. Before then, the bridge has to be rebuilt and five loads of timber have to be taken to Granville.

During the next three days, Peter and Bob replace two rotting bearers on the George Town Packet bridge and nail down new level decking; the bridge with a broken wing disappears.

The next day, I set off on foot and follow the tractor as it moves along the sandy, bracken fern-edged track. The machine resembles a giant yellow insect with four huge legs bunched up against its body. The sun is warm but the air is cold in the shadows cast by overhanging vegetation. At George Town Packet Creek, the tractor crosses the new bridge and, with the longer run-up, tows the trailer up the following slope without hesitation.

Phew.

I overtake the tractor and wave as I see the jubilant expression on Peter's face. He grins at me and waves back, but our relief soon turns to further frustration at the next obstacle – a long sandhill. The tractor gains speed in the run-up, but the engine labours, the wheels spin and fling out curtains of sand, and the vehicle comes to a standstill halfway up. Peter backs the tractor and trailer down the hill and tries again with a faster run-up. Tension grips my neck as I watch. No luck. After the third unsuccessful attempt, he accidentally backs the trailer into a deep pool of slimy mud near the base of the sandhill, where it stays, bogged, leaving the driver mad with frustration.

Together, we walk back to the farm.

The next day, Bob drives the 'dozer from the farm to the sandhill and bulldozes off some of the sand. However, when he starts towing the trailer out of the bog, the 'dozer itself becomes caught in clinging mud. My heart sinks. He swears loudly and jumps out of the seat followed by Shatzie, his dog, a black and white bitser with floppy ears and a bent tail who always rides beside him.

Bob joins Peter and me standing nearby. Together, we stare at the bogged vehicles.

'Bloody hell.' Bob shakes his head from side to side, grinding his teeth in fury. 'You know, Pete, we're paddling upstream in a barbed wire canoe, and it's full of holes.'

Utterly dejected, Peter nods as he puffs on his cigarette. 'C'mon,' he says, tossing the butt away. 'Let's get these vehicles out.'

\*

Another day has been lost. It's now impossible to have the first stockpile of timber stacked at Granville by Friday. Bob drives into Zeehan the next morning to ring the timber merchant. We're consoled by the knowledge that the hold-ups at George Town Packet Creek and the sandhill will not recur, because the problems have been fixed.

The hill at the farm proves otherwise, a permanent nightmare. Going down with a load of timber is more trouble than going up in the Land Rover has ever been. After a great deal of rain and the continual passage of vehicles, the hill has become a quagmire which not even the four-wheel drive tractor can descend without slipping sideways, often out of control until the wheels find something they can grip.

Behind the tractor is the trailer, weighed down with two tons of timber. The trailer often drops its wheels into deep, muddy ruts so that, as the tractor drags it downhill, mud piles up in front of the trailer. The men shovel this aside. On other occasions, the trailer jackknifes, sliding at right angles to the tractor and sinking into the mud. Once, the 'dozer has to be brought from the forest to push the trailer back into line behind the tractor, so they can continue their downhill progress.

Because of these hold-ups, Peter sometimes doesn't leave the farm with a load of timber until mid-afternoon. After towing it to Granville and unloading it there, he returns home about nine o'clock in the evening, exhausted.

The spring weather gods turn on weeks of drizzle. There are days of snigging in rain and deep mud and tortuous trips to Granville, as well as continuing teething problems at the mill.

We struggle on, determined to make a success of the timber venture.

\*

I'm about five months' pregnant by this time and I often feel the baby move in my swollen belly. It's a gentle sensation like a butterfly fluttering deep in my abdomen and it brings me quiet joy. However, this is a low period for me. With constant drizzle or rain, problems with the timber business and very little money to live on, I often feel dejected and yearn for a long talk with a good friend. Peter and I discuss the situation occasionally, but in the evenings, when Bob's in his caravan, we prefer to read by the fire or talk about the coming baby.

Every day, I lie on the living room floor and do my pregnancy exercises. I prop myself up on my hands and knees and tighten my abdomen, then stretch my limbs out to the front and back. Other exercises follow. I remind myself that this baby will make six people happy. For both Peter's parents and mine, it will be the first grandchild.

Unlike the men, I have the luxury of being able to distract myself from our problems. I stride across the paddocks in the drizzle, watching the cattle and listening to the bird calls in the clear air. I write stories and articles, and even dig out the half-finished children's story I'd written about the wombat that had visited our yard for a time. I edit the story, spending hours in my make-believe world. One day, I make a steamed caramel pudding, a luscious dessert that Peter and I finish off in one sitting, then groan in our chairs by the fire with overfull bellies.

My belief in the venture also sustains me. I'm certain that what we are trying to do is achievable – and that we will achieve it.

\*

Peter and I are thrilled when a friend in Zeehan, a mechanic named Otto Ortner, gives us six bantam hens and a rooster. We bring the birds out to the farm in a wire cage on the back of the Land Rover. Peter lifts the cage down onto the lawn accompanied by squawks from the occupants. Whisky takes one look at the strange creatures and disappears for the rest of the day. Always curious, the currawongs hop around the cage and study the new birds. One flies up on to the top of the cage and glares down comically at them with his head to one side. I'm excited. I'll enjoy keeping hens and gathering their eggs. Another activity to add to my rich yet simple daily life.

The bantam hens are pleasing to the eye, with feathers in various shades of brown, but the rooster is a beauty. Regal in bearing and behaviour, he struts around his harem with his tail feathers of red, green and gold held high.

'Thinks he's a king, doesn't he?' Peter says one afternoon.

'The rooster is a king.' I laugh and punch his arm. 'Where's your respect?'

Peter builds a henhouse behind the house. During the day, the birds free-range. This is good for the hens and for the eggs they produce, but not for my garden beds. I've planted fuchsias and hydrangeas around the house, and I protect the little plants with individual fences of chicken wire so the hens can't peck off leaves and scratch in the dirt around the roots. Each evening, I tempt the free-ranging birds into their night-time roost by rattling a bucket of laying pellets.

Soon after this, we buy half a dozen large white hens. The rooster's harem now consists of a dozen birds and he struts among them with his head and his tail held high, every arrogant feather proclaiming his importance. His dignity disappears when he tries to mate with the big hens, however, who peck the ground with intense concentration. When the king flies up onto the back of one of the big hens, she raises her head from the ground at this interruption and shakes her body, puzzlement on her face. What a problem to deal with when eating! Flapping noisily, the rooster balances for a moment but then slides off into a heap of feathers on the ground. Unperturbed, the hen ruffles her feathers, sets them back into place and continues with the essential task of scratching the ground.

\*

With the coming of summer, the weather improves. Problems at the mill and along the track to Granville settle down. We sell the sawn timber to the timber merchant, but there's plenty left over that's unmarketable due to knots or sapwood or size. When Peter has time, he makes blackwood bookshelves for the living room. Even the dirt floor of the little shed that houses the toilet is covered with blackwood planks. Relatives who've paid several thousand dollars for a blackwood dining table are horrified to learn that we occasionally burn blackwood in the fireplace.

One evening, Peter sits on the living room floor beside a plank of blackwood sixty-five centimetres wide. He's rubbing a rag soaked with a mixture of shellac flakes and methylated spirits along the timber. The sharp smell of metho hangs in the air.

'Look at that,' he says, leaning back and gazing at the rich, dark colouring and strong grain of the timber. 'It'll make a beautiful coffee table.'

'Yes, it's handsome timber all right.' I put down my book and add wryly, 'I'm glad we're not the only people who think so.'

The knot of worry in my stomach tightens. The income from the timber isn't enough. Peter and I are always aware of the constant difficulty of paying for food and groceries. Tank has already been put off, as we can no longer pay wages.

My husband raises his eyebrows and nods. He's worried, too, but there's something else bothering him. 'Sometimes I think we're making a mistake.'

'What do you mean?'

'We're ruining parts of the forest just to get the timber out. Is it worth it?' He looks straight at me. We've talked about this before – the ever-expanding area of destruction caused by felling and snigging. Young sassafras saplings, tiny maroon leaves from myrtle trees, tree ferns and leaf litter all fall into raw rows in the wake of the yellow machine as it drags logs out of the rainforest. 'The whole process is destructive,' he goes on. 'You cut down a tree which is a thing of beauty, then you carve a swath through the forest to drag it to the mill, then saw it into planks and flog it. There's nothing creative about that at all. If I could see the end product – a house, fine furniture – I might feel differently, but what we do is purely destructive.'

'Oh, yes.' Not only do I agree. I think about the destruction of the forest so much that I've been staying away.

'When cattle prices pick up we can stop milling timber,' I say, but I don't feel optimistic. Newspaper reports about the future of the cattle market are gloomy, and our debt to the bank is large.

'Yes, maybe,' Peter says, agreeing with my thoughts rather than my words.

We both want to stay on Top Farm. The timber allows us to do that, and we're determined to make it work.

However, our relationship with our partner continues to sour. Bob's an intelligent man and a hard worker, but Peter and I grow more and more exasperated by his carelessness. One day, he doesn't put the brake on when parking the 'dozer. He goes into his caravan for lunch, leaving the machine outside the shed. The engine's running but the clutch is unengaged.

Maintenance has recently been undertaken on the clutch, which, unbeknown to Bob, engages. Slowly but inexorably like a flow of lava, the vehicle drives itself over the paddock and down a slope, where it tips over a bank and dives onto the track below.

Peter sees the drama from a paddock and sprints across the grass to the machine. After taking one look, he runs over to the caravan and leaps inside, shouting. 'You silly bastard,' he yells. 'D'you know where the 'dozer is?'

'Eh?' Bob's been having a catnap on his tiny sofa and opens his eyes blearily. 'What's up, Pete?'

'It's gone over the bank. Landed on the blade.'

'Noooo.' Bob's eyes widen and his mouth drops open.

'Bloody idiot.' Peter's eyes are blazing and his mouth has formed a thin line across his face. 'Probably busted the hydraulic arms. They'll cost thousands of dollars to fix.'

I follow the two men as they run towards the vehicle, tilted at a steep angle over the bank.

Bob tries to laugh it off. 'Bad place to park, eh?'

Peter's having none of that. 'Bloody bastard. Why didn't you put on the brake?' he demands.

'Where's Shatzie?'

'Never mind the dog. C'mon, we've got to get the thing upright.'

The funny side is that Peter had seen Bob's dog, Shatzie, shoot off the machine like a bullet as it tipped over the bank.

The rest of the day is spent righting the 'dozer by manoeuvring the caterpillar tracks to bring the machine to an upright position on the road. Fortunately, there's no damage to the blade or its attachments.

\*

One day, I'm walking over the far paddocks of the property when I glance back towards the house and see a khaki vehicle parked outside the shed. An army vehicle? On Top Farm? I hurry home.

'Jo. Hello.'

I gasp. It's Chris Welburn, an army officer who'd married an old school friend of mine named Ann. He's stationed in Devonport on the north coast.

'Ann and I were planning to come and visit you one weekend,' he says as I lead the way inside. 'But now I see it would've been pointless bringing our sedan,' he adds with a grin. 'I'm looking for an area where I can undertake some adventure training for my men. The terrain and the track out here are ideal for difficult driving training. Could we use it?'

Astonished, I nod. 'Of course.' Whatever next?

I fill the kettle and light the gas stove.

'I met Peter on the track,' Chris tells me. Peter had left with a load of timber for Granville that morning. 'He'd just blown a tyre on the trailer. I gave him a hand with it.' With a rueful face, he adds, 'Soon afterwards, we got bogged.' So even the army gets bogged! 'He pulled us out.' Chris sighs and frowns and leans back against the kitchen bench. 'And now my truck's stuck at a different place. One of the creeks. The one with a steep slope turning down to a ford.'

'George Town Packet,' I say, spooning coffee into two mugs.

He nods. 'My men are there trying to get it out. We came down the first section of that slippery slope with no trouble, but when the driver turned the corner, the back took off. Slid straight into a ditch.

We tried to jack it up and edge it out – even towing it with the Land Rover – but it wouldn't move.'

'The big tractor should be able to pull it out, but Peter won't be back there until late this afternoon.'

'Hope we've got it out by then.' He pauses, peering through the kitchen window. 'Where's the sawmill?'

I point inland towards the rainforest. 'You can't see it from here.'

I notice Chris's impeccable manners as we carry our mugs of coffee into the living room and sit down. He opens the door for me and doesn't sit until I do. He's keen to learn about our timber business. While we talk, I admire the extraordinary sight of a smart army uniform in a room that knows only scruffy farmers who are often unshaven, muddy and in need of haircuts.

That evening, Peter doesn't return until nine o'clock. I'm worried but should have known better.

'Been helping the army put a hole in their grog supply,' he tells me. 'Good bloke, Chris,' he goes on, peeling off his raincoat in the alcove. 'Reckons an exercise for his men'd be driving the trucks up here, loading them with timber, then driving back to Granville.'

'What?' I stand still and stare at him. 'The army's going to cart timber for us?'

'Yep.' My husband grins, brimming with bonhomie. 'All I do is tell him the date. As long as it fits into his adventure training schedule, he's happy to do it.'

Heedless of his muddy jumper, I grab him and give him a big hug. 'That's fantastic!' To have someone step in and offer to transport our timber to Granville at no cost is a real fillip, as though Fate has decided to give us a break.

'Whoa there.' Always the practical one, Peter brings me down to earth. 'This is a one-off, sweetheart. It doesn't mean we'll be out of the woods financially.'

'Of course not. But it'll save days of carting.' I calm down and slide his meal out of the oven. *And it's already raising our spirits.*

\*

Another old friend of mine comes to stay for a week just before I'm due to fly to Canberra. Gill Davidson is tall and gentle and loves animals. Together we feed the hens, walk all over the farm and talk non-stop.

One day, Gill and I ride the motorbike down the hill and along the track to a spot where an encroaching sand dune has cut off the old track to the Pieman River. Propelled by prevailing winds, the sand dune has travelled over the land, smothering tea tree, bracken fern and all the other vegetation in its path, leaving only their tips poking above the surface to gaze upon their vanishing world.

We reach the base of the ten-metre-high dune, park the bike and begin to climb up the slippery dry sand. The dune is so steep that on each step I slide back down to the previous one. Puffing and giggling like girls, we eventually reach the top and turn around and slide down to the base on our bottoms. Exhilarated, with my hair flying and my gumboots filling with sand, I turn around and do it again. So does Gill.

We kick off our gumboots and tip out the fine, dry sand. Refined sand, eons old. I still for a moment and gaze at our ancient surroundings. We're the only people in this wild country, and the crashing of waves on the beach beyond the dune is the only sound.

\*

A couple of days later, I become aware of a heavy, dragging sensation in my abdomen. I'm seven months' pregnant, fit and healthy, and I ignore the discomfort as Gill and I prepare an evening meal of beef stroganoff and rice. The next morning, Peter waves goodbye as we set off with Bob in the Land Rover to drive to the north coast. Gill and I will stay the night with him and his wife at Oldina, then catch the plane to Canberra the next morning at Wynyard airport.

Before dawn the next day, I awake in one of the Werners' spare beds with a tight sensation around my pregnant belly. Immediately alert, I jerk upright in the darkness and put my hand on my abdomen. The muscles are as tight as a steel band. Contractions. My mind reels. I don't want this baby born yet. It's way too early.

Slowly, the room lightens with the coming dawn. The Werners' cat keeps me company, purring beside me while I try to stay calm. When Gill wakes up, I tell her what's happening and give thanks she's a midwife. She checks me over and makes me lie down after I dress while she packs my suitcase. At breakfast, I ask Bob to drive us to the hospital, not the airport. Poor man, he nearly chokes on his toast and liverwurst.

An excruciating pain in my back keeps me squirming in the seat in Bob's car as we drive to Burnie hospital. The kindly doctor is Scottish. He has grey hair and wears bifocals and a tartan bowtie. When I tell him where I live and describe our track, he frowns and nods.

'That's it, lassie,' he says. 'That rough road of yours. That's brought this on.'

*It wasn't only the road.* I stare at the ceiling as his gentle hands examine my belly.

He gives me Valium to calm the muscles of my uterus and tells me I'll be staying put for a couple of days. The drug does the trick and I'm dopey for the rest of the day.

# 11

# The army comes to Top Farm

My hospital bed in Burnie looks through a window onto green lawn and flower beds. I'm in a double room with a woman named Rachael who's just given birth to her third child. I'm embarrassed about my untidy hair, which needs a cut, and the state of my clothes. My elastic-fronted makeshift slacks are shabby and my long, thick, cosy dressing gown is grubby. I've been waiting to wash it in my parents' automatic washing machine in Canberra, but now it lies across the foot of my bed for all the world to see.

'You're so unorganised, Jo,' Rachael says. She's just given birth to a baby girl after two boys and is feeling pretty chuffed with herself. 'I'm glad I didn't see you on your wedding day.'

At that moment, I'm rummaging in my handbag for paper on which to write Peter a note, as Bob is heading back to Top Farm that afternoon. (Later, my husband tells me the words I scrawled on a scrap of paper did nothing to reassure him I was okay.) I look up and peer at her as she sits on the side of her bed. Wedding day? What's she talking about?

'Oh, no,' Gill protests, indignant on my behalf. 'Jo was very organised then.'

Dear Gill. I feel tearfully grateful she's with me. My threatened premature delivery has upset her plans, too. She rings my parents and changes our flights. She's staying with Bob's wife and comes to the hospital every day.

Once the crisis is over, the doctor tells me I can get up the next day but not fly for another two. I spend a lazy couple of days, reading and talking to Gill and other patients and the friendly staff, although on the second day I'm brought up short. Rachael stands up, and a large drop of bright red blood falls onto one of her pink slippers; unlike my clothes, her pink satin slippers are shiny and new. The drop of bright red blood is a stark foretelling of what's in store for me.

Excruciating back pain and bright red blood. I dread the coming pain when I deliver this baby, but at least that is, now, once again, two months down the track. All being well.

Gill and I meet the hospital's resident psychologist, a young woman called Laurann.

In between seeing patients, Laurann sits beside my bed and darns colourful striped socks. 'I hope you and your bulge reach Canberra intact,' she says when we say goodbye.

We do. I see the relief on Mum's and Yang's faces as, still in one piece, I emerge with Gill from the plane at Canberra airport. I begin two months of relaxed life in my parents' home.

I'm pampered by doting grandparents-to-be and enjoy long conversations with friends, but after a few weeks I find that suburban living is so cramped. Nowhere can I escape the sight of next door's washing flapping in the wind, the sound of their children arguing and shouting, the smell of their food cooking. Instead of birdsong and the distant boom of the surf, I hear so many intrusive noises – traffic, telephones, television. I find myself longing for the spaciousness of open paddocks and the peace I've grown to love.

In Canberra, I enjoy the luxury of standing under a hot shower without having to boil the water first, and experience a deep and refreshing sense of relief to be away from Top Farm worries. However, I miss Peter, and I wish I could tell him the weird and funny things that I experience because of the pregnancy. Whenever I pull out the cutlery drawer to lay the table, the drawer hits my bulging belly and the forks, knives and spoons rattle and slide about in their compartments. I can't see my toenails, let alone cut them. I wish he could place his hand on my hugely swollen belly and feel the baby kicking, and watch the baby's toes – or are they fingers? – rippling across my bare skin.

Imagine my shock when Yang tells me he won't let me drive because I'm pregnant. 'Darling, it's not safe for you to be behind the wheel. I'll drive you wherever you want to go.'

I stare at him and begin to disagree, at the same time trying to show my gratefulness to him and Mum for potentially lending me the car. But Yang is adamant. So he drives me to friends' places and to coffee shops, and picks me up later. I am twenty-five years old, have held a driving licence since I was seventeen, and have travelled around the world, sometimes on my own, but he won't let me drive because I'm *pregnant*.

I tell myself I should take it as endearing rather than restrictive. If only Peter were with me. We would have laughed together over this ban, and he would have helped me to see the funny side (if there was a funny side).

My doting parents hardly let me do anything. I long for Peter, who would expect and encourage me to, for instance, work in Mum's vegetable garden. 'You're pregnant, not sick,' I can hear him saying.

\*

I walk to the Weston shops and back every day and go shopping with Mum for nappies and other baby necessities. I'm in awe of the baby clothes she's knitting. Little cardigans in soft cream wool and a huge wool shawl that will be as warm as my poncho. She's also sewing nighties in cream flannelette and decorating them with embroidered flowers.

I devour every sentence of Peter's letters. He writes that with the dry summer weather, milling and carting timber are going on with few hitches. Prices for the timber are good. He's eating a lot of baked wallaby while I'm away and likes it. He also tells me he's pulled several holiday-makers out of bogs, but wasn't able to help a fisherman who'd become bogged on the beach. The incoming tide had rolled his vehicle over and filled it with sand. Just like that.

There doesn't seem to be a dull moment down there. As I sit in Canberra, idly contemplating my navel, which is sticking straight out like a dead tree on a hilltop, I feel I'm missing everything. In his next letter, Peter tells me about the army exercise. He writes that Chris and his men arrived in two khaki Land Rovers and six four-wheel drive khaki trucks. By the time the soldiers pitched their khaki tents about half a kilometre from the house, it looked as though war had come to the west coast.

The next morning, Peter, Bob and the men loaded timber on to two of the trucks and the convoy set out for Granville. Peter went along on our four-wheel drive tractor. The dry weather meant sand was the main hazard and, sure enough, the last two trucks couldn't make it up the long yellow sandhill because the sand had already been gouged deeply by the other trucks. This was the spot where Bob had bulldozed sand away some months before.

Peter positioned the tractor in front of each truck in turn, hitched up the chain, and hauled them up. At Granville, Chris and his men pitched their tents while Peter loaded the timber onto the waiting merchant's truck. Later, he made his way home fortified once again by the army's alcohol.

Peter learns more about Bob during the army's visit, another side of our partner that's not to our liking. One day, they ask the visitors to have lunch in the house.

'Only the officers, Pete,' Bob says.

'No.' Peter groans. 'You're a bloody snob, Werner.'

All of the visitors have lunch in the house, especially after Chris tells Bob they always stick together as a group.

Another black mark against our partner.

*

During a regular visit to my gynaecologist very late in the pregnancy, I learn he will be on holiday when the baby is due. His fingers are firm and gentle on my belly. 'Would you like to be induced before I go?' he asks in a casual voice. 'Or are you comfortable with having a different doctor, if the baby comes when I'm away?'

What an extraordinary question! I stare up at him in surprise. 'Oh, yes, any doctor is fine,' I say bluntly. I'm shocked and indignant at the very idea that the timing of my baby's birth could depend on a doctor's *holiday*. 'I want the baby to come just when it's ready.'

*

Lying on a bed in the labour ward of the Royal Canberra Hospital, reading a book called *Darwin and the Beagle* by Alan Moorehead, dealing with each uterine contraction by conscientiously doing the breathing exercises I'd practised daily on the living room floor in the Top Farm cottage, I reckon I'm handling this delivery caper pretty well.

Until my waters break and all hell breaks loose. I cry out as a fierce pain seizes my body. Darwin falls to the floor. Nicola is born four hours later, on the very day the doctor returns from his holiday.

The telegram telling Peter about our daughter's arrival sits in our post office box in Zeehan for three days before he finds it. Immediately, he books a flight and flies to Canberra the next day. Mum and Yang meet the plane and drive him straight to the hospital.

My husband strolls into the ward. I'm so thrilled to see him, and I admire his lean, strong body, jet-black hair and the expression of love on his face as he gazes at me. I think how smart he looks in his best slacks and his sports jacket.

We kiss and hug tightly, and I bury my face in his shoulder. I lead him into the nursery, where about thirty babies lie in hospital cots. I gather up our baby and pass her to him.

His eyes widen with uncertainty but his arms hold her securely. 'She's so tiny,' he whispers, peering down into Nicola's little face.

'No, she's a good weight,' I say. 'Seven pounds and seven ounces. But she's lost a bit since birth. They all do, in the first week,' I add with all the authority of a new mother.

'She's healthy?' he asks as he unwraps the baby blanket and counts her tiny fingers and toes.

'Oh, yes. She's been checked by the doctor.'

I stay in hospital for a week until breastfeeding has settled down, then we take Nicola home to Mum's and Yang's place. Peter stays for a few weeks, weeks packed with feeds and nappy changes. Nicola was born in the middle of December, so Christmas and New Year come around soon afterwards. We accept an invitation to a New Year's Eve party, taking Nicola in a hand-held bassinet. I feed her during the party in the darkened bedroom of our friend's house, and I feel pretty chuffed – I've given birth to a baby two weeks before and here I am able to go out and talk and laugh and dance.

Ah, how naïve and ungrateful I am! Although my nights are disturbed because I'm feeding Nicola, I'm not bowed down by exhaustion, because Mum makes sure I'm spared any housework. She does all the cleaning, shopping and cooking, although I wash our clothes, of course, and the nappies.

After Peter leaves to return to Top Farm, Mum and Yang continue to spoil me. Yang insists on doing the washing up every night. 'No, darling,' he says after dinner. 'You'll be feeding Squidge soon.' 'Squidge' is the pet name he's given Nicola early on, and I smile whenever I hear it.

When I'd been pregnant, I'd chafed at the restrictiveness of not being able to drive. Now that Nicola has arrived, I'm thoughtlessly unappreciative of all the help Mum and Yang give me. I even have the time and energy to write an article about an intriguing configuration of two intertwined Huon pine trees, one estimated to be an astonishing thirteen hundred years old, on a forested bank in Macquarie Harbour. The information had been given to me by our friend Peter Jones on the north coast, and I'd tucked it into my suitcase before leaving Top Farm. My piece is later published in *The Canberra Times*. Finding out things and writing about them is one of my favourite activities, especially when my words are published, for then I know they will be read.

*

I'm eager to return to Top Farm and decide to go when Nicola is about two months old, but I take her to a pediatrician first. I tell him about the farm's remoteness. He smiles and says, 'Babies survive most things.' I like to think he gives the go-ahead because he sees I'm a competent mother, but a couple of Canberra matrons are not so sure. 'What if your milk dries up?' they ask. As I resemble a milking cow at the time, I find this very funny. What's more, for the first time in my life, I have a cleavage – but I'm hardly in a position to show it off in a low-cut ball dress.

I feed my little daughter behind a pillow on the Fokker Friendship aeroplane droning across Bass Strait. When the plane touches down at Wynyard airport and I glimpse Peter waiting outside the tiny terminal building, I know I've made the right decision. The cool wind of northern Tasmania greets me as I step down from the plane with the baby in my arms. The aches of separation vanish as he encloses both of us in a big hug. Families are made to be together.

We drive straight to Zeehan and stock up on supplies, then head out towards the coast. The bright yellow flowers of parrot pea and gorse border the track. Their colour matches my yellow jumper that is rapidly becoming grubby in the workaday Land Rover, but I don't care. While Nicola sleeps in a baby sling across my chest, I revel in the familiarity of the wild, restless landscape: the buttongrass plains, the old mine workings along the track, the huge tree ferns growing in the pockets of rainforest through which we drive. After four months' absence, my first glimpse of the wild rocky coast is stirring. Even on this calm day, a heavy, five-metre swell is coming in. The fresh salty fragrance of the sea mingled with whiffs of rotting seaweed remind me that I am back in the real world after a four-month sojourn in the unnatural perfection of Australia's capital city.

The real world, indeed. On the track ahead we see a familiar west coast character peering into the bonnet of a battered, four-wheel drive vehicle parked in the middle of the track.

'G'day, Richo,' Peter says as we climb out of the Land Rover and join him on the road.

Richo has a thin face and grey hair and grey clothes, all of which match his grey Land Rover. He lives with his brother in a corrugated-iron house on Zeehan's outskirts. I remember a story about him. While visiting Conical Rocks some months before, he'd tried to drive over a large boulder partly buried in the track, but his vehicle had bellied on top of the boulder with its front wheels off the ground. It would have been possible to change into reverse and back off, but his reverse gear had long since packed it in. He'd walked all the way back to Granville, where he'd talked someone into driving him back up to the Conicals to tow his vehicle off the rock, in return for several cans of beer.

Today's problem is different. He'd come out to the coast for a spot of fishing, but, after an argument with a relative, he'd leaped into his Land Rover and turned the ignition key with too much anger-induced strength. It had broken off in the keyhole.

'I fixed it with a piece of wire behind the ignition. She started and made it to here,' he says, swearing under his breath.

'Then conked out,' Peter puts in.

'Yeah.' As he wipes a hand across his forehead, I see that even the hairs on the back of his hand are grey.

Peter turns our vehicle around and hitches up the chain to pull-start Richo's. Every time he engages the clutch to start the engine, the vehicle jerks violently but refuses to start. Then, with a grinding squeal, the bumper bar breaks off, clattering along the road behind our Land Rover.

'That heap belongs at the tip,' Peter says.

'Yeah. Bloody thing.' He takes a couple of cans of beer out of a carton on the front seat and hands one to Peter. 'I'll camp here tonight. Maybe I'll get a lift in the morning.'

During my absence, a whole section of the Zeehan–Granville track has been re-routed by the Zeehan Commission. The road now skirts the eastern or inland foothills of Mt Heemskirk. Previously, the track from Zeehan had reached the coast at Trial Harbour and followed the coastline north to Granville. The alteration shortens the distance between Zeehan and Granville and cuts out an awful stretch of coastal track that's narrow and bumpy with lots of short, steep pinches. The new track reduces our travelling time by at least half an hour.

Soon after leaving Richo, we drive through thick forest then cross the Heemskirk River on the only bridge I've ever seen that turns a corner. We emerge into open heath country and more buttongrass plains, where the track becomes a white quartzite road nearing 'highway' standard. In places, we're able to speed up to forty kilometres per hour.

Wildflowers colour the vegetation at every turn. In this harsh country where the elements are extreme, I'm always surprised that many of the wildflowers are small and dainty, such as the climbing blueberry, the boronia and the leatherwood. I notice a clematis twirling its delicate vine and cream-coloured flowers over bracken fern along the edge of the track.

A dozen sulphur-crested cockatoos take flight from the branches of a dead gum, their raucous calls splitting the air. For the hundredth time I wonder why Nature decrees these enchanting creatures should have such a screeching call.

We pass through Granville and bump along the track, the familiar sound of the gear changes telling me I'm home. I talk non-stop to my husband, who says I can slow down now that I'm back in the country.

I'm tired from the long journey and eager to reach home, but excitement gives me energy. Also, I want to show off my baby. Peter stops outside the Bigwoods' neat blue cottage. Elsie and Rolly Bigwood are market gardeners who sell their produce to the shops and pubs in Zeehan. We yarn over the fence. Nicola is sleeping on my chest but she attracts many compliments from Elsie, who always calls me 'Duck'. Elsie's front garden is a mass of dazzling flowers. Cornflowers, poppies, dahlias, godetias and carnations. She gives me some cuttings and I stow them in the carton of groceries on the back of the Land Rover.

Viv Coleman's shack lies further along the track. We stop there to say hello and give him the newspaper and supplies he'd asked Peter to pick up in town. After knocking on the door and hearing an answering bellow, we step into a back room that contains laundry tubs, drums of fuel and a litter of kittens curled up on a hessian bag. We find Viv in the main room. The walls and cupboards are bright yellow and a cast-iron kettle sits on top of a blackened wood stove set into one wall. A colander, a beater and a sieve hang on nails on the wall. Paperback novels sag along a high shelf.

Old Viv roars a welcome and, without apology or embarrassment, says, 'I'm a bit liquored up, m'girl. If you don't mind that, then come on in, come in.' He pushes a brown terrier off a chair and beckons me to sit down.

I like old Viv, a big man with wisps of hair and bright eyes who's dressed in a brown jumper and old trousers. He'd been a miner in Williamsford all his working life. During World War Two, Viv was in the Australian army and fought against the Japanese at Buna on the north coast of PNG, not far from the cocoa plantation on which Peter had grown up.

He peers down at Nicola in my arms. 'So this is the babe.'

She's awake now, trying to put her small fist into her mouth, which it somehow always misses. Viv smiles, a smile that starts around his mouth then spreads to his eyes and all of his face. He and his wife had raised ten children in Williamsford, a small mining hamlet in the mountains near Rosebery. He's now the proud grandfather of twenty-three children and great-grandfather of another four.

Gently, the old man takes Nicola in his arms and rocks her for several minutes. After passing her back to me, he slaps his left breast with his right hand. 'Are you feeding her on the tit or the bottle, girl?'

I blink. If only the Canberra matrons could have heard that! 'Oh, well, um – she's breastfed, Viv.'

Old Viv roars his approval and gives Peter and me a beer each, pouring mine into a glass. 'It's good for the milk, girl. You eat the right things and care for your baby. Stick with your man, too. Stick with him with patience and understanding. Peter is your man and you're his woman. Your destiny lies up there on Top Farm.'

As a west coaster who's known Top Farm all his life, Viv is pleased the farm is being worked by a young couple who plan to stay.

During a repetitious conversation packed with goodwill and Viv's assertion that we'd 'make a go of it up there', I feed Nicola and change her nappy. As we are leaving, Viv insists we take some of his vegetables – silverbeet, marrows and carrots.

We climb into the Land Rover and head north along the track with the fragrance of fresh vegetables filling the cab of the vehicle.

# 12

# Bareback no hands

When we reach home late that afternoon, I'm thrilled to find that Peter has built shelves and a cupboard in the bedroom as well as a large change table for the baby.

The next morning, he leads me to the fertiliser shed. When I step in the door, I gasp with surprise and pleasure. A twin-tub washing machine stands against one wall. No more washing by hand. Above the washing machine he's installed a tap attached to the end of a long black polythene pipe running over the ground from the water tank behind the house. Power is supplied by a bright orange electricity cable slung from the eaves of the house across to the new laundry. At its lowest point, the cable swings a couple of metres above the ground and is to be the cause of a hilarious equestrian mishap some months later.

I'm thrilled to be back home, to watch sleek, healthy cattle grazing on our pastures, to hear the calls of the plovers as they wheel in flight over the paddocks, to hear the sound of the horses galloping for the sheer joy of it, to smell the aroma of tomatoes picked in the garden, and even to chop kindling for the fire. Although it's late in February and supposedly the height of summer, we often need a fire to warm the house.

Nicola sleeps in a bassinet at the end of our bed. It's a solid, wicker bassinet painted white that's been lent to us by Sydney relatives, Norma and John Barrett. Norma and John are aunt and uncle to both Peter and me. Weird, isn't it?

Norma is my father's sister, and John is Peter's father's brother. Peter and I had met each other through Auntie Norma. When I was about to head off to PNG in January 1970 for a three-week trip around the country with a friend, Auntie Norma said to me, 'Joanna, you must go and stay with John's brother, George. He and his family live on a cocoa plantation in the Northern District.' So, with my friend and travelling companion, Judy Colwell, I did just that.

George and Phyl Barrett had three sons, Bruce, Peter and Ian. The young men gave us a tour of their cocoa plantation and processing plant, took Judy and me tramping through the bush to a nearby village and swimming in Sambogo swimming hole, and we all danced the night away in the Popondetta golf club on New Year's Eve.

Judy and I left the plantation and travelled on to the PNG highlands and the tropical paradise of Madang, then returned to Canberra. Six months later, I again headed to the exotic, tropical land north of Australia, this time on my own, and began working in Port Moresby. There, Peter and I met up again as he was working in Moresby, too.

\*

Fast forward to Nicola's birth and Auntie Norma's offer to lend us the bassinet she had bought for her own babies many years before. The bassinet has travelled in the hold of the plane on the flight across Bass Strait. On the first evening back in the little cottage on Top Farm, when I lay sleepy Nicola down in the bassinet, I remember Auntie Norma telling me that both Peter and I had slept in it as babies.

I blink and stand still. This must have happened when our respective parents were staying with Norma and John at their home in Sydney at different times. I try to imagine Peter and me, as babies, each sleeping in the bassinet over twenty-five years before, and shake my head in bewilderment.

Listening to Nicola's snuffling noises as she settles down to sleep, I tuck her in and marvel at the time warp and bizarre coincidence, all rolled into one. The presence of the bassinet at the end of our bed reinforces my feeling of belonging in the family, even though I'm living in this remote cottage on the west coast of Tasmania. I smile to myself with quiet joy.

\*

In the dry summer weather, sawmilling has been proceeding apace, and carting timber along the troublesome track has been easier than in winter. Prices for blackwood are high. The cash flow keeps the bank at bay. Thankfully, Bob has been pulling his weight in the partnership and there have been no more mishaps with machinery. Things are looking up.

Now that Peter and I have a baby, I am doubly glad Bob lives in the caravan, although he still joins us for occasional evening meals. As a new little family, we need privacy to settle down into our new life. Adjusting to parenthood is a major undertaking. I discover there are many situations that arise which are baffling, especially in the foggy tiredness of new motherhood. I worry when Nicola cries for no apparent reason. There are days when a feed takes several hours and there are still dirty nappies in the bucket and a meal to cook. At other times, I can't seem to get rid of the rash on her little bottom.

Peter helps when he can, but he's working seven days a week. Like most babies, Nicola wakes frequently at night for feeds and nappy changes. Like many husbands, he becomes a remarkably heavy sleeper. 'What's the point of my waking up? I can't feed her,' he says with crushing logic.

Ever curious, the cattle are keen to identify the unfamiliar sound that blasts from the house whenever its newest occupant cries. From all over the paddocks, they canter up to the fence and line up, eyes alert and ears forward. After I feed Nicola, I take her outside to show them, but, as she is by then quiet and content, the cows and steers are left none the wiser about the noise.

The nights are very cold, so I put mittens on Nicola's hands to keep them warm. One night, one of the mittens slips off and in the morning her little hand is icy cold and slightly swollen. I'm startled and concerned, even though the skin is still a healthy pink. I pick her up and cuddle her and warm up her hand as I feed her. My daughter doesn't seem worried about her cold hand. All she wants is the 'milkbar', as Yang calls me when I'm breastfeeding.

\*

Not long after I return to the farm with Nicola, we learn that Brian Jago has been drowned. He'd bought a fishing trawler in Hobart and had taken on two nephews as crewmen, one of whom was Tank, the young man who'd worked for us. The men were sailing the trawler around to the west coast, up into Bass Strait and on to Devonport. However, the trawler was caught in a fierce storm about twenty-five kilometres north of Top Farm. Huge waves battered the vessel and pushed it on to the rocky coast. Only one man survived. Tank. After thirty-six hours on a lonely beach, he was found cold and exhausted among the few bits of timber that were the ship's only remains.

The tragedy saddens us a great deal. Brian had lent us his rotary hoe. He'd caught fresh crayfish for us on many occasions. Most meaningful for me, he'd given me tea in a chipped, pink china cup. Brian was a real 'rum 'un', an abalone diver and cray fisherman who'd often told friends he'd never become cray bait. 'The sea won't get me,' he'd declared.

His body was never found.

\*

When Nicola is about four months old, Shatzie gives birth to pups under the house. She's chosen the spot well: on the dirt next to the base of the chimney where the puppies are warm and sheltered. Cute as they are, with their tightly shut eyes and ballooning tummies, the puppies' whimpering disturbs the human baby above and exasperates me, because Nicola starts crying, too. This in turn sets the pups to louder whimpering and brings Shatzie running back from the paddocks. We mothers feed and comfort our little ones until they settle down. I try to laugh. It is funny.

Whisky shows great interest in the pups, which doesn't please Shatzie. Never Whisky's friend, the dog, in her new role as a protective mother, declares him an enemy. Previously, Shatzie had felt the pain of many scratches from Whisky's claws, but now the situation is reversed. Three times, the dog chases the cat all the way over the front paddock to the far creek. Poor Whisky. He's receiving less attention from me now, too. Although he remains a loved pet, Nicola's arrival pushes him firmly into the background.

As for the pups, Bob takes Shatzie and her family to Oldina when the puppies are about three weeks old, much to my relief. And, no doubt, to Whisky's.

A pink toy that plays Johannes Brahms's 'Lullaby' hangs from a nail in the bedroom. Whenever I put Nicola down in the bassinet, I pull the cord hanging from the toy and tiptoe from the room, letting the gentle melody soothe her to sleep.

With no telephone, no doorbell and no deadlines for anything except meals, I have plenty of time for cuddles with our little daughter. My days are filled with feeds and washing and caring for Nicola. Every morning, I bath her in a baby bath on the dining table. Together, we have fun splashing the water, while nappies hang on a clothes horse in front of the fire to dry.

I become totally absorbed in Top Farm domesticity. It's late summer by now. Hydrangeas and fuchsias are flowering in the garden bed in front of the house and every day I pick fresh produce in the vegetable garden. Zucchinis, cabbages, cauliflowers, carrots, tomatoes. Sometimes I carry Nicola outside in a baby sling across my chest and at other times I potter in the vegetable garden while she sleeps. I pull out weeds growing among the raspberry canes, pick the late beans and cut rhubarb stalks.

On other days, while she is asleep, I grab the chance to write a letter to a friend – except on those occasions when I'm so tired that Brahms lulls me to sleep, too.

Despite the fact that before shopping days I always check our supplies and write a shopping list, there are times when I forget to buy something and could do with a corner shop; running out of salt is no joke.

Abalone is one of the foods we eat on the west coast that needs plenty of salt, or plenty of something. Anything, in fact. One Sunday afternoon, we hear the familiar roar of a vehicle coming up the hill. It's Frank Mihalovich, the caravan park owner and crocoite miner who gave us some of the bricks for our fireplace and chimney. Accompanied by his children and a couple of friends, Frank has come to say hello and bring us several abalone.

'Ever tried them?' he asks me, as he reaches into a metal box on the back of his Land Rover and brings out several shellfish the size of bread and butter plates.

I shake my head.

'Caught this morning.' He opens his penknife and prises open one of the molluscs.

A heavy, salty smell rises into the air. I put out a finger and press the mustard-coloured flesh. Wet rubber, that's what it feels like.

Over cups of tea and coffee inside, Frank tells me how to cook abalone. 'Slice it thinly, then fry it for thirty seconds in butter and lemon juice. Only thirty seconds. Any longer and it'll be as tough as old boots.'

Old boots? My cooked abalone is as tough as ancient boots. The flavour is good, however – a result of the butter and lemon juice, I reckon. Later, I read an article in a newspaper about cooking this shellfish, which is a delicacy in parts of Asia. If you don't want to take risks, the article advises, cook the abalone on a low heat for a long time, either steaming for three hours or pressure cooking for one hour. So, some weeks later when we are again given abalone by a pair of generous abalone divers, I try the slow cooking method, but have no more success than the previous time. I dish up tough rubber, and sigh. Fate is telling me this apparent delicacy is not a dish I ought to cook.

*

Winter is soon upon us and brings drizzle, rain and cold winds for weeks, but one night there's a heavy frost. We awake to see pastures and paddocks swathed in crisp whiteness. I go outside to explore and the grass crackles underfoot. Because we're near the sea, we rarely experience frosts, but this one is so severe it freezes the water pipe into the house and kills the tomatoes.

These are small prices to pay for the sunny days that follow. The glare of the sun is so strong that I dig out my sunglasses which I haven't worn for months. I neglect the inside jobs and spend most of the time outdoors with Nicola. Carrying her in the baby sling across my chest, I walk over the pastures and sit with the cattle and watch the ducks on the dam. We often tramp over to the sawmill, where the dry weather is allowing the men to turn out plenty of milled timber every day.

One morning, I lie on the lawn in the house yard while Nicola crawls over my legs and stomach, slipping and tumbling off and giggling with the fun of it all. She stops to examine the grass, pulling the blades through her fingers. I turn my face up to the sun and close my eyes. I feel like hugging the warmth. It seeps into me, caressing me deep down as though heating my bones.

Whisky appears and Nicola tries to grab his ear. The cat rolls on the grass and plays with the tiny uncurling frond of a bracken fern plant growing among the grass stalks. He cuffs it with a paw, but, like a boxer's dummy, the frond keeps swinging back to him and he cuffs it again, and again. Nicola laughs, a baby chuckle of pure joy. She crawls on the grass, eats grass stalks and chases butterflies, her plump cheeks glowing pink and her white blonde hair blowing in the breeze. Utter contentment fills me.

While the dry weather is a boon for sawmilling, the short winter days mean there are fewer hours in which to snig the logs, mill them and cart the sawn timber to Granville. Peter and Bob are cutting large blackwood logs at this time, most of which are sawn into flitches, long lengths with sizeable dimensions such as twenty centimetres by fifteen.

We're all pleased with the weather and the good price for timber, but not with the endless trouble carting the sawn planks to Granville. Something is always going wrong. One day, it's the four-wheel drive tractor's left-hand rear tyre, flat because the inner tube is rotting in places. With a new tyre no closer than Burnie, Peter and Bob decide to take one pack of timber to Granville on the Land Rover and three on the trailer hauled by the small Fergie tractor.

Easier said than done.

Weeks of dry weather have merely turned the track on the hill from sloshy mud to potter's clay. (Peter has long since scouted around on the other slopes below the farm in a futile search for an alternative route.) The Fergie inches down the steepest section of the muddy hill while towing the trailer loaded with timber, but the trailer slides sideways and rams the timber into one of the back wheels of the little tractor. The tractor stops dead, refusing to budge, forwards or backwards. The men curse and try to manhandle the trailer away from the wheel, but it's impossible.

'Bloody hell,' Bob says. 'I'll have to get the 'dozer.'

He walks back to the forest and drives the bulldozer across the paddocks to the hill. The big machine quickly straightens the trailer, taking the pressure off the Fergie's wheel. The little tractor is able to continue down the hill, hauling its precious load. It's already lunchtime and no timber has yet reached Granville.

Late that evening, the men return in the two vehicles, having deposited four bundles of timber at Granville.

\*

I'm so absorbed in my daily life that if visitors arrive unexpectedly, I immediately become aware of the hole in the old jumper I'm wearing or the cobwebs hanging in a corner of the kitchen. When I'm self-conscious or embarrassed, I talk too much, which gets me into more strife.

This happens one day when two strangers arrive at the farm, a couple in a Land Rover. I ask them into the house for tea or coffee, but I'm embarrassed about my messy kitchen, in which I've been trying out a new recipe for vegetable soup. Potato peelings and onion skins are scattered on the bench together with a couple of wooden spoons, and dirty sieves and saucepans lie in the sink. I find myself telling the couple the story of a mouse that drowned overnight in a jug of milk I'd left on the kitchen bench. I'd discovered the mouse floating in the milk early that morning. (Now, many years later, I still don't know why I left a jug of milk out of the fridge. Was our tiny refrigerator already full up? Was the night so cold it didn't matter if the milk was left out?)

I pause for breath.

With a shiver of distaste, the woman says, 'Eeeww, that's disgusting.'

She's dressed in a lavender mohair jumper teamed with tailored white slacks. Her pearl drop earrings swing back and forth as she talks. I'm surprised at her attire (Pearls! When four-wheel driving on the west coast!), but these thoughts are swamped by my much bigger worry. Our workaday kitchen looks smaller and dingier than ever with this smartly dressed woman standing in it and peering at the meat safe. I try to hide the hole in the side seam of my jeans.

'I had to fish him out with a tablespoon. I felt so sorry for him,' I rush on. 'He was limp and his fur was very milky. And how did he get in anyway? The jug's made of china, so the sides are smooth. Maybe he was climbing on the shelves above, and lost his grip, and fell in.'

Her husband coughs and gazes at me with wide eyes. He says nothing about the mouse, but they scarper soon afterwards.

Outside, holding Nicola as I wave goodbye, I kick myself for everything – telling the mouse story, wearing jeans that need mending on the one day in weeks when visitors arrive, chattering non-stop, feeling embarrassed about things that I should not feel embarrassed about.

But as their vehicle disappears over the crest of the hill, my embarrassment subsides and I become aware that my main feeling is one of disappointment that I hadn't been able to ignite any enthusiasm in them for Top Farm.

Back in the house, I put on the kettle and laugh at myself. The unlikely story of the drowned mouse hadn't been the best one to tell, but the episode will amuse Peter when he comes in.

\*

I have no such problems with a couple who come to stay one weekend in spring. Sue and John live in Zeehan, where Sue is one of the nursing sisters at the health clinic and John works at the Renison Bell tin mine just out of town. We've become acquainted during our infrequent trips to town and have arranged a visit. Peter will give himself a rare weekend off.

He meets them at Granville on Saturday morning and they all arrive at Top Farm in time for lunch. No mohair jumper and pearls here. Sue wears jeans with a windcheater, John a flannel shirt with trousers and boots. His moustache is cropped and neat and there's a twinkle in his eye whenever he laughs. Sue is more serious. Rarely smiling but extremely observant, she asks about my Mexican bookends and even notices the Vegemite jar of faeces which Bob still insists on keeping behind the books.

Her eyes widen when I tell her the story. 'You're joking. A thylacine?'

I explain that Dr Guiler says no, the faeces aren't from a thylacine, but Sue is showing the excitement that all Tasmanians feel when there's talk of the supposedly extinct animal.

Over a hot dish of salmon and macaroni mixed into cheese sauce, served with fresh salad from the garden, we find that our visitors are interested in everything we're doing on Top Farm. They're easy guests. With all the stimulating talk and activity that afternoon, I forget I have a cold and want to fall into bed. I hold Nicola on my lap as we bounce over the paddocks in the Land Rover to Newdegate Creek, show them the intricacies of the sawmill and take them walking in the rainforest. We reach an old surveyors' camp which Peter and I have visited previously.

'Look over there,' says Sue, pointing to a tree towering over the camp. 'See that tiny piece of white sticking out of the trunk?'

We hurry over. Some of the sapwood of the tree has rotted and fallen away, exposing a hollow in the trunk. We're all astonished when Peter pulls out a Hobart newspaper dated 1922 that had apparently been crammed into the hollow. Most of the pages are completely dry and many of the edges are brittle but it is intact.

'Who could have left it here?' John asks.

'The surveyors,' Peter says. 'Tells us they were here in 1922.'

A frisson of excitement speeds up my spine. I think of those men in 1922 who had, unsurprisingly, brought a newspaper out to their camp and had probably sat on a log and read it after a day's work in the bush. I can't wait to examine the fifty-four-year-old paper. We all marvel that it's survived for over half a century inside a tree trunk.

Back in the house, we spread out the pages on the dining table, trying not to tear the brittle edges. The paper rustles as we flatten the creases, and the smell of old newsprint hangs in the air. We all pore over the columns of small print, intrigued and chattering, reading aloud the news items and advertisements. There's an item headed 'Dinner Jackets for Women – Freak Fashion in Paris'. Beside it there's an advertisement for white honeycomb quilts for the price of five shillings and eleven pence. (Five shillings and eleven pence would be, literally, fifty-nine cents in today's money, but in 1922 this amount would have bought far more than fifty-nine cents would buy today.)

I marvel that the west coast continues to throw fascinating tidbits of history in my direction, adding to my interest in this unique part of the world.

While Peter takes John to the stockyards the next morning, Sue and I wander around the garden. In the bed running along the outside of the vegetable garden, my fuchsias are blooming. Their delicate flowers are ballerinas dancing among the leaves. I keep an eye on Nicola crawling on the ground.

Sue is pensive. She gazes all around, turning slowly towards the sea, the forest and the distant mountains. 'You're so far from anywhere out here, Jo,' she says at last, looking at me with an intense gaze. 'So isolated. What do you *do* all day?'

I'm astonished. I gaze back at her, unable to speak. My mind bulges with vivid images – bathing Nicola, chopping kindling, sitting among the cattle, picking strawberries, watching a wombat by torchlight, feeding Nicola, exploring the tidelines along the beach, writing stories, admiring a robin swaying on a grass tussock, reading beside the fire, painting the front door, picking fresh vegetables – but I can't think of any words with which to answer her question.

I'm nonplussed and talk it over with Peter that evening. Evidently, Sue has never lived in the country and doesn't know how full the days can be on a farm – and when caring for a baby. But I like both John and Sue. Their enthusiasm and interest in what we're doing on Top Farm is a morale-boosting shot in the arm. Despite my bad cold, I awake next morning feeling refreshed and enlivened by their visit.

\*

Because of the demands of the timber, the cattle have been neglected, but they can't be put off any longer. Peter and Bob set aside a weekend to deal with them, asking Johnny and Colin Casey to help. A mate of theirs comes along too, a horseman called Nick who works for the Renison Bell tin mine. He appears over the brow of the hill on his horse and is every bit a real cowboy. Stetson hat, high boots and a big silver buckle on his belt. Even a fringed waistcoat.

After catching Big Mick and Pinto with scraps of bread, the Caseys mount and join Nick. They gallop off to round up the cattle from the far corners of the property. Peter rides our motorbike and Bob takes the Land Rover. As the animals are driven towards the stockyards, the Caseys' dog, Jacky, races back and forth behind them and nips the stragglers on the ankles to encourage them to rejoin the mob.

Nicola and I watch from the house yard, then follow the mob to the stockyards. Once all the animals are inside the main holding area, a few are put into the race, a narrow fenced corridor which leads into the bail. The bail is a framework which holds each animal's head securely.

Nicola and I watch the action from the tray of the Land Rover, leaning over the roof of the cab. My daughter is as interested as I am, her eyes wide as she tries to take everything in. The air is filled with shouts from the men and bellows from the beasts. Peter, Bob, Colin, Johnny and Nick work as a team as they deal with the animals one by one. The cattle aren't used to being handled, so they heave and jostle each other, roaring their distress with frothy mouths and huge eyes. Once in the bail, each animal is drenched for worms by having a squirt of liquid from a big syringe poked into its mouth; dabbed with a blue liquid to kill lice (it's a systemic so will spread throughout the body); and ear-tagged. The bull calves are castrated. All the animals have their tails bobbed to show they've been done.

The men are continually on the go, leaping up and down the fences to keep the cattle moving through or dealing with the animal in the bail. The two bulls, like the professionals they are, submit to the unwanted attention quietly, but the Hereford steers rebel. They throw their heads back and jump and buck, and a few even turn a half-circle within the confines of the narrow race.

Four of them even manage to leap over the side of the high fence of the race, quite a feat with no run-up. Unluckily for them, they find themselves back in the holding area of the stockyards. Soon afterwards these four are back in the race where, with sheer brute strength, the men force each of them in turn into the bail.

\*

On a Sunday several weeks later, the Caseys and a couple of mates, Dick and Mackie, give us an unforgettable afternoon. Peter and I lead a supposedly quiet country life, but we're treated to a unique show that's so exciting it has me perched on the edge of my seat. The men arrive with two cartons of beer and a metal file half a metre long.

'Gonna give the horses a manicure,' Colin tells us as he jumps down from the vehicle brandishing the file. 'Got to have a beer first.'

Colin has a hearty manner and, when he's surprised, his trademark turn of phrase is 'strike me pink'. As always, Johnny is thoughtful. He knows I don't like beer so he's brought along a bottle of lemonade with which I can make a shandy.

The brothers' links with Top Farm go back a long way. Their father,

Peter Casey, had helped clear the farm in the early 1900s when it was owned by Dave Nicholas. Dave used to buy two or three hundred head of cattle in Smithton in the north, walk them down the coast, swimming them across the Arthur and Pieman Rivers, and fatten them on the farm. Later, the animals were slaughtered and the meat sold in the Nicholases' butcher's shops in the west coast mining towns.

After a few beers and lots of talk, Johnny and Colin catch the horses in the paddock and bring them into the house yard. Big Mick stands quietly as Colin runs his hand down each of his legs in turn and, bending over the hooves, files away the long growth. Pinto's turn comes next.

After the manicures, Colin slips up onto Big Mick's back and, with a beer in one hand and the mane in the other, canters around the yard – along the front fence, past the corner post where Whisky holds court with the cattle, up the side fence, behind the house and down along the fence of the vegetable garden. He has to duck to pass under the orange electricity cable strung between the house and the laundry.

Peter has built a balcony at the front of the house out of eucalypt planks and I sit on the edge, legs dangling. Nicola sits on my lap, watching everything. Johnny, Peter, Mackie and Dick sit either side of me, sipping their cans of beer.

'A bit slow, Colin,' shouts Peter, egging him on. 'Any slower, you'd be going backwards.'

Grinning, Colin snorts and trots up to the balcony. He hands his beer to Mackie before riding Big Mick around the circuit again, faster. He spurs the horse into a gallop and goes around again, even faster, then again and again. Because of the small area of the circuit, the horse and rider are constantly leaning inwards.

Shouts of 'Whoopie' and 'C'mon, Colin!' fill the air.

Big Mick is a powerful horse. Watching him gallop at full stretch is a spectacular sight. With his mane and tail streaming out, he speeds around the circuit with the man on his back. With each circuit, Colin becomes more daring, even letting go of the mane and stretching his arms to the sky.

Eventually, he slows the big horse down and jumps off. Big Mick stands a metre in front of me, his chest pumping as he shakes his massive head. With his horsey sweat in my nostrils, I feel part of the action, an exhilarating feeling.

'Your turn now, Pete,' Colin says, getting even.

After my husband's tame circuit, Johnny downs his beer and leaps onto Big Mick. Soon, he's galloping around the yard at a greater speed than even Colin had managed. I gasp each time Johnny and the horse explode from behind the house, going so fast they're almost a blur. Little Nicola's eyes are riveted on the speeding horse each time it goes past. She laughs and chuckles, her head swinging from side to side as she watches horse and rider disappear around one corner of the house, then erupt from the other.

And still Johnny urges Big Mick into a faster gallop, holding his hands up high. Bareback, full gallop, no hands. What a sight!

He slows Big Mick down, jumps off and swaggers over to the balcony. 'Thirst's gettin' to me,' he says.

On his next turn, Colin takes Mackie with him, doubling up on the big stock horse. Mackie is one of the younger Zeehan cowboys who reckons there should be hitching rails outside the pubs and shops in town. 'There's nowhere to tie your horse,' he says to me that afternoon, truly perplexed.

After a couple of circuits, Colin lets Mackie off and goes on to do the best act of the afternoon. We think Colin has the measure of the orange electricity cable swaying in the air between the house and the laundry, but on his next circuit, with Big Mick galloping beneath him, he's upon it before he has time to duck. The cable catches him under the chin and, for a heartbeat, holds him. Just in time, he flicks his head sideways and slips free.

When he dismounts and ambles over to the balcony, walking bow-legged and rubbing his neck, he's ribbed mercilessly.

'Going blind, Colin?' asks Peter.

'You should've somersaulted off backwards, mate,' Mackie tells him.

'I thought you'd hung yourself back there,' Johnny says, laughing, while Dick claps Colin on the back and Mackie opens a beer for him.

'So did I,' says the cowboy. 'Strike me pink, that was close. Strike me pink it was.'

## 13

# A thylacine in the forest?

Soon after this, Nicola catches a cold, her first. Snuffling, unable to suck properly because of her blocked nose, she cries and cries, blocking her nose even more. I rub Vicks onto her chest to help her breathe, but she is worse the next morning. We take her into the doctor in Zeehan, who prescribes antibiotics for the infection in her chest.

Back home, she wakes more often than usual at night. I grow tired and catch the cold too. Feeling exhausted, sick and miserable, I make a quick job of cleaning up the living room one morning. Using the dustpan and broom, I sweep up the worst of the dirt on the floor and a few petals that have dropped from a vase of flowers, as well as a bullet that's fallen from a shelf and is lying beneath the petals. I throw the lot into the cold fireplace.

That evening, I light the fire then chop up onions, carrots and leftover meat. Fried with leftover rice, that will do for dinner. Bone weary, every muscle aching with tiredness, I plonk gratefully into a chair in front of the fire. Peter comes in and sits down. Nicola is lying in her bouncinette, smiling and gurgling. Her cold is getting better, thanks to the antibiotics clearing up the infection in her chest.

An explosion rips the air.

I jerk upright. So does Peter.

'Sounded like a bullet,' he says, looking at me, puzzled. 'But how –'

Oh. Oh, God. A cold hand slides around my heart.

My husband's eyebrows shoot up as he sees the expression on my face. 'Did you – did you put a bullet in the fireplace?'

I nod, unable to speak. I look at Nicola kicking her little pink legs on her bouncinette only metres from the fire. Horror fills me. I can't breathe.

'Only one?'

I manage to nod.

He looks around the room. 'There's no hole in the wall or ceiling,' he says, matter-of-factly. 'It must have gone off in the ash drop.'

Peter says very little but I sense his anger at my stupidity. He kneels in front of the fire and spreads out the pieces of burning wood, putting out the flames and checking for any more bullets, just in case.

I slump deeper into my chair. I feel like curling up into a ball and not facing the world for a millennium.

No sleep for me that night. I squirm as I lie in bed thinking of all the unspeakable 'what ifs'. I give desperate thanks for the ash drop.

\*

A couple of months later, Bob races back to the house at lunchtime, his expressive face bursting with excitement. 'Jo, you'll never guess what I've found,' he says, eyes shining and eyebrows raised. 'It's a dead wallaby that's been killed by a thylacine, I reckon. Beside a snigging track. The chest's been ripped open and some of the soft parts have been eaten.' He peers at me intently. 'Remember what Eric Guiler said about the way a Tasmanian tiger kills its prey?'

I nod. This is exciting news, indeed. Dr Guiler had told us that thylacines ripped open the chest cavity of a wallaby and ate only the soft organs.

Bob runs off to his caravan for a quick lunch. Peter and I down our sandwiches, then we all hurry to the rainforest. Peter carries Nicola but I take along the baby sling in which to carry her home afterwards.

Bob leads us to a snigging track about a kilometre from the sawmill. We follow the track through a patch of dogwood into the rainforest. The forest is quiet and hushed, and the sweet fragrance of myrtle and sassafras trees hangs in the air. We pick our way over the forest floor as Bob leads us to a small stream. On the bank of the stream, moss and leaves and colourful fungi are heavily shaded by tree ferns and the higher forest canopy. On a slope just beyond a shaft of sunlight lies the carcass of a Bennett's wallaby. The animal has been slit cleanly around the throat and under the left forepaw, leaving the paw hanging by only a shred of skin. I smell fresh meat as I peer into the exposed ribcage of the animal. The heart has been eaten but the lungs and liver appear to be intact. We look for footprints in the vicinity but can't see any. After taking one sniff, Bob's dog, Shatzie, bolts away from the dead animal. Strange – but significant? We don't know.

My heart thumps with excitement as I adjust my footing on the uneven ground. Are we really looking at a kill made by an animal that's thought to be extinct?

'I'll write to Dr Guiler,' I say.

'What about some photos?' Peter says. 'There's a film in the camera.'

I walk back to the house and return to the carcass that afternoon and take several photographs.

The next day, Bob goes back to the dead wallaby. The soft parts of the animal have been finished off but not the rest of the body. By a thylacine? A devil would have eaten the lot.

Some time later, I hear back from Dr Guiler. He's interested in our find, but non-committal. Many sightings of thylacines in various parts of Tasmania have been reported over the years, but until one of the animals is captured on film or in a cage, there can be no confirmation of its continued existence.

The following evening, Peter and I eat wallaby for dinner. I stuff the hindquarters with a mixture of onions, herbs and breadcrumbs then bake it in the camp oven hanging over the fire. The fragrant heat of the wallaby rises into my nostrils as I dish up our meals. The flavour of the meat is strong and gamey and the unfamiliar texture fills my mouth pleasantly. Peter had eaten wallaby several times while I'd been in Canberra and enjoyed it. I like it, too, and we eat it baked and stewed every so often after that.

\*

My gazanias begin flowering early in summer. Elsie Bigwood had given me the cuttings some time before and I'd planted them in the garden bed at the front of the house. I love their bright colours. Apricot, bronze, gold, orange and yellow. I often cut a dozen blooms and arrange them in a vase and place it in the centre of the polished timber dining table.

Every arrangement I create is different, depending on the configuration and length of the stems, the number of leaves and the colours of the petals. I usually manage to achieve an interesting, if not a totally pleasing, shape. Standing at the kitchen bench, absorbed in my task, holding the stems that are already in the vase with my fingers, I think of nothing else. I often surprise myself when I stand back and gasp with pleasure at the arrangement I've created.

There are days when I'm out walking on the property with Nicola and I pick wildflowers, even weeds such as fireweed, and arrange them in a vase. Arrangements created by my own hands give me quiet pleasure and I smile to myself whenever my eyes fall on them. On days when our financial worries hang in my head and threaten to overwhelm me, I know that arranging a vase of flowers will push the worry into the background.

The vegetable garden continues to give Peter and me great pleasure. I often take Nicola into the garden when I'm planting new seeds or seedlings, and weeding. She helps by pulling out weeds growing on the paths between the beds – and she tip-prunes every plant in sight.

I remember a time during our first summer when we were establishing the vegetable garden and planting seeds. Thrilled with the garden, I'd nevertheless felt a sensation, an emotion, that I couldn't identify. It kept disappearing as soon as I focused on it, like trying to hold a bubble in your fingertips. As soon as you think you've got it, it's gone.

I touch Nicola's soft hair and realise the sensation had resulted from an absence. I'd wanted a child with me in the garden. A thrill of profound joy and fulfilment pulses through me. My hands are dirty but I pick up my daughter and hug her, breathing in her baby smell, the smell of new life.

Nicola is having none of it. She squirms to be put down again so she can go on playing in the dirt. I grin and muss her hair.

## 14

# From landed gentry to garbage man

Our financial situation continues to deteriorate. Income from the sawmill pays bank interest and covers running expenses like fuel and machinery parts, but that's all. Our savings have dwindled to nothing. There's always pressure to get more blackwood out and thus more money in, so the men work long hours with little time off – except on those days when Bob stays away from the farm for longer than planned, which brings milling to a standstill as two men are needed in the sawmill. His extended absences have been occurring more often in the last few months. Deeply frustrated, Peter continues with many essential farm jobs, but resentment grows in both of us at Bob's cavalier attitude. Getting blackwood out is the one and only activity that brings in desperately-needed money.

We know that if the weather gods are kind to us and the dry summer weather continues – and if Bob stays on the farm – more timber will be going out in the coming months.

The question is: can we wait?

Around this time, a young Tasmanian devil starts hanging around the house, attracted, I guess, by the smell of meat drifting outside. The creature lollops around the yard, sniffing, so I throw it a chunk of wallaby meat and lower myself onto the grass to watch. Devils are normally nocturnal animals, so I'm thrilled to be able to study this one in the daytime. It quickly devours the meat, eyeing me as it chews and gulps. The next day, it's back, so I toss a few chicken scraps onto the lawn and once again sit down to watch.

I know it's a juvenile because it's smaller than a fully grown animal and its fur is shiny and smooth, with no areas of skin where tufts of fur have been ripped out during fights.

The young devil becomes a regular visitor and I always give it something to eat: crayfish shells or fatty bits from our meals. My little devil grows so tame that, one day, it comes up to within half a metre of me on the grass, staring up at me and sniffing the air expectantly. I give it a piece of wallaby meat. A few days later, to my astonishment and delight, the creature creeps up the steps onto the balcony and scratches at the door.

Thrilled as I am, I'm not going to let a devil inside the house. I continue to feed it on the grass away from the balcony, excited to be so close to this wild creature as it eats and chews and swallows, occasionally glancing at me with alert eyes. I'm so close I could put out my hand and pat it, if I were silly enough

*

It's ironic that on a sunny day in February when the weather is at its most benign, Peter and I make the decision to leave Top Farm. The business can't support us. There isn't enough timber going out, and cattle prices are still at rock-bottom. We have no money left to live on. When a situation is as stark as this, the decision itself is easy, but despondency grips both of us. We're sitting at the dining table and talking in sombre voices.

'That's it, then.' Peter stands up and moves to my chair and pulls me to my feet.

We hug each other for a long moment. The end of our Top Farm dream.

The next step is to give our partner the news.

We're expecting Bob to return to the farm that day, a Monday, but it's not until the following Friday that the vehicle roars up the hill. I am anxious, frustrated and angry. Peter, too. We've run out of cereal and cheese, soap and honey, and most other supplies are low. With no fresh meat, we've eaten wallaby for dinner on too many nights. Yet my emotional reaction to Bob's absences goes far beyond these practical concerns. I feel betrayed and dismayed and vulnerable. Let down, out of control and resentful. I hate being dependent on someone else. Waiting day after day for Bob to return eats away at my well-being and creates an uncomfortable looseness in my stomach.

'He was due back four days ago,' Peter says on Thursday afternoon. He's holding Nicola in the kitchen. She's gripping a red toy in her little hand and banging it against the kitchen bench, grinning with the noise she's making. He sighs. 'We've made the right decision.'

Dusk is settling over the paddocks when Bob arrives late on Friday afternoon. Inside the house, we're both sharp with him as we tell him what we've decided. We're standing in the kitchen and Bob puts on the kettle. I'm stirring an egg and milk custard mixture in a saucepan over a pan of hot water for Nicola, while she plays with her toys on the living room floor.

'I see,' he says, his face dropping. However, he understands our position and suggests we write to a businessman friend of his in Sydney asking him to take over our share of the partnership. Land, assets, and debts.

Bob makes himself a cup of coffee and, after taking a sip, leans back against the kitchen bench. I'm relieved when he and Peter move into the living room. I fetch Nicola and hold her warm and sturdy little body on my hip as I stir. My thoughts race on and I become lost in the fragrant, gently swirling liquid in the saucepan, which sends a sweet smell into the air. It's been largely our under-estimation of the effects of the climate on our timber venture that has brought us to this point. And the poor track. And rock-bottom cattle prices. And, I'm finally prepared to admit, our initial under-capitalisation.

*

The focus for Peter and me shifts from Top Farm to the vital task of finding him a job, although it's to be three more months before we drive away for the last time. In the meantime, work at the sawmill continues as usual – when Bob is there. I avoid his company, but Peter has to work with him and the two manage to have a cordial relationship.

Although our decision brings its own relief, dismay catches me unawares at times, too, when I'm picking wildflowers in the bush, or feeding my little devil, or fossicking among the driftwood and shells on the beach for objects for another still-life.

Top Farm has given me an injection of confidence. As an only child and a girl, my role in the family when I was growing up had been a passive one. I was brought up to be a good girl, to be nice to everyone and always to do what I was told.

My experiences have muted the feelings of inadequacy I felt early in our sojourn on Top Farm, during the visit of our English friends. I have a new inner strength, a personal identity, a sense of well-being that's resulted not only from my rich daily life, but also from pursuing a worthwhile goal, even though it's proved to be elusive. Working towards that goal with every ounce of my energy, dealing with all the joys and pitfalls along the way, has given me a new feeling of self-confidence. Simply coping has often prompted a temptation to punch the air and shout, 'I can do it!'

On Top Farm, I've lived in the most immediate present and my experiences have awakened a deep satisfaction that's come from doing things, even if it's only growing peas and painting the front door. I've learned to laugh when I'm tired, and never, ever, to forget to buy salt at the supermarket.

\*

One day, I dig over the soil where I'm going to plant dahlia tubers that Don Smith's mother, Mrs Beryl Smith, has given me during a visit to Zeehan. I can't let the tubers die, even if I never see them flower. I begin the task feeling gloomy, but as I turn over the dark soil and breathe in the fragrance of moist earth, my mood lifts. With my fingers, I form holes in the earth for the tubers and begin to feel calmer about the situation. Soon we'll leave. So be it. We don't know where we'll go or what we'll do. Well, so be that, too.

You never know what's around the corner. Soon after this, Peter is offered a job by the chief conservation officer in Tasmania, David Steane. A job with an *income*. We'd met David when he'd called in to the farm some time before on a working visit to the west coast, studying the sand dunes to see if they needed stabilising. He's well known for his dune reclamation work along the coast of northern Tasmania. He now thinks Peter will be ideally located to take on several tasks around Granville Harbour: stabilising the sand dunes by planting particular species of grasses and upgrading the track between Granville and Top Farm for holidaymakers and campers. We'll be paid for the use of our bulldozer on the track.

Peter accepts the job, although it means milling only at weekends. My sense of the ridiculous is tickled by the prospect of my husband being paid to do up the awful track which has helped to thwart our timber venture. It's a crazy world.

The day before Peter is due to meet his parents in Zeehan to bring them out for a three-week stay over Christmas, he finds himself relocating the Granville rubbish dump and picking up beer cans along the foreshore between Duck Creek and Granville. 'From landed gentry to garbage man,' he quips.

Phyl and George Barrett arrive from North Queensland with a suitcase full of summer clothes: shorts, shirts, dresses, sandals. Within twenty-four hours, we're lending them jumpers, cardigans, coats, socks and slippers.

'It's summer, Jo,' Phyl says. 'I didn't think it would be so *cold*.'

George is a practical person who's interested in everything, so when he isn't at the sawmill or walking hand-in-hand over the paddocks with Phyl, he's in the shed building a cot for Nicola out of our beautiful blackwood timber. Hand-polished and large enough for a two-year-old child, the cot was still being used several years later by our second daughter, Robyn.

Phyl helps me and plays with Nicola. On sunny days, we often sit outside on the grass. Phyl has a lovely laugh, a real *joie de vivre* laugh, and to hear her laughter and Nicola's baby chuckles together is a delight. She tells me her feelings about the west coast. 'It's so wild and isolated here, Jo. As we drove along the track from Zeehan, I found the wilderness overwhelming, like a force you couldn't fight against. All those bleak plains. The sea roaring on to rocks. Then a steep rise up to the farm, and suddenly ahead was a little house with an air of contentment and peace about it.'

I'm surprised to hear this from a woman who, with her husband, pioneered a cocoa plantation in the Papuan jungles in the 1950s. I remind Phyl of their isolation, boggy roads and rickety bridges, but she waves away my words with a laugh. 'Jo, that was different.'

*

Johnny and Colin Casey invite us to their New Year's Eve celebrations at Granville Harbour. A party, a rare treat. We're keen to go. Phyl and George are happy to babysit Nicola. The party is to be held on the grassy slope in front of the Caseys' shack. Being a typical summer's evening, it's freezing, so I dress in my warmest clothes. Slacks, a skivvy, a jumper, a beanie, gloves, thick socks and boots, and my llama-wool poncho that encloses me like a woollen tent.

We set off in a party mood and reach Granville at dusk. Peter parks the Land Rover outside the front fence. Johnny and Colin's land is virtually a paddock where their horses are barred only from the vegetable patch out the back. As we walk up the dirt path from the gate towards the shack, I see two horses standing at the side of the building, swishing their tails and watching the newcomers. A large keg of beer stands on the veranda, where old stools and blocks of wood serve as seats. Viv Coleman is there, as well as a tall, square-faced Rosebery miner named Harry who'd introduced us to green ginger wine the year before, a potent west coast favourite.

With a shandy in hand – once again Johnny has thoughtfully remembered to buy a bottle of lemonade for me – I talk to the people I know and meet those I don't. As the temperature drops, my toes change from warm to cold to numb, but I enjoy myself as I stand near the huge fire burning on the grass in front of the shack. Johnny's swarthy features are lit up by the firelight as he builds up the blaze with massive logs. He introduces me to a young miner from Zeehan who's wearing a red and yellow checked lumber-jacket. After this, the evening gets out of hand. The lumber-jacket is fascinated by my poncho. He asks endless questions about llamas in general and the poncho in particular, and insists on fingering the fluffy fringe around the border. I sip my shandy and smile politely. Finally, he says he wants to hug the llama, and keeps chuckling at his own joke. I reckon this is an old line and look around for Peter.

As midnight draws near, no one links arms and begins to sing Auld Lang Syne. Oh no, nothing as tame as that on the west coast. When the midnight pips sound over someone's transistor radio, two shotgun blasts explode over our heads. I jump, shocked, not at first knowing what has happened. My eyes pick out a figure crouching on the ground near the gate, one arm holding a shotgun, the other tilting a can of beer up to his mouth. Angry shouts from Colin and Johnny blister the air.

Too much for me. I thank the Caseys and grab Peter, who's already had the same idea. After hurried goodbyes to our apologetic hosts, we climb into the vehicle and speed off, only slowing down after we've turned a few corners.

## 15

## Three tiny rosebuds

Peter posts letters seeking a job to every possible employer. Towards the end of the conservation job, he takes a couple of days off to go job-hunting in Burnie, accompanied by Nicola and me. Our long-term aim is to save enough money to buy another farm in north-west Tasmania in a couple of years.

In Burnie, we stay at a little motel on the north coast near Wynyard, whose friendly owner makes it more of a bed and breakfast place than a motel, reminding me of those in which I'd stayed in England and Scotland. Petite, dark-haired Mrs Stevenson keeps three guest rooms. Her living room is cosy with thick carpets, polished timber furniture and lace antimacassars on the backs of the easy chairs. She welcomes us into her home at any time to watch television or read the paper.

The employment officer at Australian Pulp and Paper Mills tells us there might be a job for Peter with their forestry section in Tasmania. This doesn't come to anything, but the following week, several days after we've returned to the farm and Bob has arrived with the mail, Peter opens a letter to find he's being offered a job at the APPM sawmill at Cape Rodney in PNG. It doesn't take us long to decide that returning to PNG would be a backward step.

Besides, there's a possible job at the Renison Bell tin mine near Zeehan, the mine that was established in 1959 and brought a new wave of prosperity to the town. I wonder how dangerous underground mining will be, but console myself by thinking it's probably no worse than felling huge blackwood trees in the forest and working in a sawmill. Peter hears about the job from Frank Mihalovich, the crocoite miner.

'The mine manager told me they're looking for someone,' Frank explains to him in Granville one day. 'The pay's good but it's shift work. You'll have to go underground first to see if you can handle it. Some can't.'

One afternoon after a day's work along the coast, Peter drives to the mine. The mine manager, Bobby Clark, takes him underground in a Land Rover and they drive along many kilometres of underground roads.

When he arrives home on Top Farm for a very late meal, I badger him with questions. 'What was it like? Did you feel claustrophobic?'

'No,' he says, shaking his head. 'Just lost. Completely disoriented. It's a foreign world down there. Humid and all in darkness except for the lights on the vehicles and the ceiling lights. They're attached to the pipes running along the tops of the tunnels.'

He eats as he talks. 'I was given a cap lamp to wear, but I didn't know how to use it properly. It never seemed to point to where I wanted to look. Huge ore trucks roared past and there were loaders in the stopes. Overhead pipes were everywhere, running along all the roofs of the tunnels.'

'What sort of pipes?'

'All sorts. They take electricity and fresh air in and pump water out.'

'Sounds like a world of its own.'

He nods. 'In some spots crib rooms have been blasted out of the rock. They're like caves, with tables and benches set up.'

'D'you think you could work down there?'

Peter shrugs and nods. 'All I'll be doing is driving an ore truck and carting ore up from the stopes. Although for the first couple of months, I'll be at the wheel of a Land Rover –' he pauses, grinning wickedly, expecting a reaction from me '– delivering explosives to the men in the stopes.'

'Explosives.' I groan. Out of the frying pan into the fire.

Late one afternoon, Peter is doing our shopping in Zeehan after a day's work at Granville when a man hails him outside the Central Pub in the main street.

'You've got that job,' he says. It's Grant Clark, son of Bobby, the mine manager. Grant is a shift boss at the mine.

The pay is good. Peter will have to become accustomed to shiftwork. I will, too. Day shift one week, evening shift the next and night shift in the third week. Two weeks out of three I'll be cooking our main meal in the middle of the day rather than in the evening. It will be a different way of life but we're cheerful and optimistic; there's nothing like the promise of a regular income to cheer the soul when you've had none for two and a half years. We're allocated a two bedroom, semi-detached company flat in Renison's housing estate in Zeehan. We've already heard that Bob's business friend in Sydney has agreed to take over our share of the partnership.

*

Things move quickly after that and soon it's our final day on Top Farm. After packing the last of our belongings, I walk outside to the climbing rose that Peter brought home for me from Zeehan over a year before. I gasp in surprise and wonder. The little plant has struggled to survive but now, on our last day, it's produced three tiny flower buds. Bending over, I gaze at the beauty of the miniature rosebuds and wipe my wet eyes. The little rose will be on its own from now on.

So will the young Tasmanian devil. As Peter, Nicola and I drive away from Top Farm for the last time with our furniture and suitcases loaded onto the back of the Land Rover, I look back and my heart jags. My tame devil is standing on the balcony of the house, gazing after us.

As we drive down the hill with the vegetation at the sides of the track brushing against the vehicle, my main feeling is one of utter relief. From now on, we'll have the luxury of money coming in regularly. Yet deep down, dismay creeps outwards from my bones. I've grown to love our life on the isolated farm at the end of the track.

And Peter? He wishes we didn't have to leave. Top Farm, the setting, the work, the daily life, suited him down to the ground.

In the cab of the Land Rover, we look at each other. The expression on Peter's face mirrors my own emotions. Disappointment and resignation mixed with relief and hope. I smile ruefully and squeeze his arm. Whisky sits in a box at my feet, and fourteen-month-old Nicola is on my lap. I sigh and kiss the top of her blonde head as Peter changes gears beside us and the vehicle bumps down the hill.

I turn my eyes to the track ahead and a tamer life in a mining town.

# Notes

1. David Davies, *The Last of the Tasmanians*, Shakespeare Head Press, Sydney, 1973.
2. T. Jetson, *It's a different country down there: A history of droving in western Tasmania*, Smithton, Tasmania, Circular Head Bicentenary Project Team, 2004, page 57.
3. Ibid., page 3.
4. Geoffrey Blainey, *The Peaks of Lyell*, Melbourne University Press, 1967, page 18.
5. My mother was referring to Black & White Scotch Whisky.
6. In recent years, the population of Tasmanian devils has been decimated by a facial tumour disease. Captive breeding of these unique carnivorous marsupials is being undertaken at a number of facilities in Australia.
7. The origins of this ditty are unknown.

www.ingramcontent.com/pod-product-compliance
Lightning Source LLC
Chambersburg PA
CBHW071452080526
44587CB00014B/2080